The Red Cross's Public Health Turn

The Red Cross's Public Health Turn

The Cannes Medical Conference of 1919 and the Origins of the League of Red Cross Societies

Romain Fathi

ANTHEM PRESS

Anthem Press
An imprint of Wimbledon Publishing Company
www.anthempress.com

This edition first published in UK and USA 2025
by ANTHEM PRESS
75–76 Blackfriars Road, London SE1 8HA, UK
or PO Box 9779, London SW19 7ZG, UK
and
244 Madison Ave #116, New York, NY 10016, USA

© 2025 Romain Fathi

The author asserts the moral right to be identified as the author of this work.

All rights reserved. Without limiting the rights under copyright reserved above,
no part of this publication may be reproduced, stored or introduced into
a retrieval system, or transmitted, in any form or by any means
(electronic, mechanical, photocopying, recording or otherwise),
without the prior written permission of both the copyright
owner and the above publisher of this book.

British Library Cataloguing-in-Publication Data
A catalogue record for this book is available from the British Library.

Library of Congress Cataloging-in-Publication Data: 2025931863
A catalog record for this book has been requested.

ISBN-13: 978-1-83999-434-0 (Pbk)
ISBN-10: 1-83999-434-7 (Pbk)

Cover image credit: Pictorial Record of the Medical Conference held at Cannes,
France, April 1 to 11 1919 at the Initiation of the Committee of Red Cross Societies
(Geneva, Switzerland, 1919), IFRC Archives, Box Z000363.

This title is also available as an e-book

CONTENTS

Acknowledgements		vii
Introduction		1
1	Tectonic Shifts in the Red Cross Red Crescent Movement	11
2	Justifying the First Humanitarian International Public Health Organisation	25
3.	An American Initiative or a 'Natural Evolution' for the Red Cross Movement?	35
4.	Knowledge is the Cure	45
5.	Designing the Organisational Structure of the Red Cross's Peacetime Body	57
Conclusion		69
Appendix		77
Bibliography		83

ACKNOWLEDGEMENTS

This small book is one of several publications that have resulted from an Australian Research Council grant to investigate the work of the League of Red Cross Societies (DP190101171). That research project comprises exceptional team members with whom it has been a real delight to collaborate with: Melanie Oppenheimer (lead), Susanne Schech, Neville Wylie and Rosemary Cresswell. We have been on this journey for quite a number of years now, and it has been a privilege to work with and learn from such generous and talented colleagues, and I sincerely thank them.

There is still so much to find out about the League of Red Cross Societies, what it did and did not achieve since its foundation in 1919, and how it fits within the expansion of humanitarianism in the twentieth century. On this note, our team will publish a larger monograph next year, so watch out for its publication. I hope that both works will inspire some of you to deepen our investigations into the League and the Red Cross Red Crescent movement's history.

You don't write history without sources, and I am deeply indebted to three remarkable and outstanding archivists at the International Federation of Red Cross and Red Crescent Societies (IFRC): Grant Mitchell, Mélanie Blondin and Sarah-Joy Maddeaux. Their support and knowledge of the resources held in IFRC archives, alongside lunchtime chats and their constant enthusiasm, have been integral to the making of this book. If you write on the Red Cross Red Crescent movement and can make it to Geneva, the IFRC's archives and its library are a wonderful place to work. Besides the somewhat solitary endeavour of historical research, I have enjoyed the conferences that our team has been able to organise at the IFRC, and meeting colleagues from all around the world on these occasions. For me, this has turned the headquarters of the largest humanitarian network into a place of academic exchange, collegiality and collaboration, with discussions often continuing further down the road at the Café du Soleil.

The IFRC is located a short walk away from the archives and library of the International Committee of the Red Cross (ICRC). There, a number of people have also been generous with their time and knowledge. I would like to thank Fabrizio Bensi, Daniel Palmieri, Cédric Cotter and Charlotte Mohr. Staff whose names were not revealed through the research process at the National Archives at College Park, the Hoover Institution Library and Archives, the Bibliothèque Nationale de France, and the Diplomatic Archives at La Courneuve are not forgotten. They too have enabled me to put pieces of the puzzle together.

This book has three homes: Flinders University, which generously funded and supported this research alongside the Australian Research Council; the Centre d'Histoire de Sciences Po, always a terrific and truly stimulating research environment to write and exchange with colleagues; and the Australian National University in Australia's bush capital, where I moved more recently. Besides the research project's team members, I have been blessed with the wonderful support of terrific colleagues who have made a contribution to this book along the way through their encouragements, a comment made at a seminar, a morning or afternoon tea conference break, historiographical recommendations, and thoughtful reading and editing of drafts. I will never be a native English speaker and so I am especially grateful to those of you who have assisted with the latter. Thank you, Malcolm Allbrook, Alessandro Antonello, Aditya Balasubramanian, Joshua Black, Marie Cugnet, Matthew Cunneen, Jean-François Fayet, Matthew Fitzpatrick, Prudence Flowers, David Forsythe, Sam Furphy, Emily Gallagher, Irène Herrmann, Julia Irwin, James Kane, Catherine Kevin, Michael McGuire, Ann McGrath, Maria Nugent, Guillaume Piketty, Annmarie Reid, Paul-André Rosental, Robert Saint, David Romney Smith, Zoe Smith, Michelle Staff, Martin Thomas, Virginie Troit, Jess Urwin and James Watson.

Naturally, I am grateful to family members and my partner in life, Claire Rioult, for their unflinching support, patience and love.

INTRODUCTION

When sighting a red cross or a red crescent on a white flag on a mast, a ship, a truck, or an armband, almost everyone would instantly identify the emblems of the Red Cross Red Crescent movement.[1] They are symbols of protection that epitomise the most identifiable humanitarian network of all. That network is also the largest of its kind, with a Red Cross or Red Crescent national society present in 191 of the 193 countries that are member states of the United Nations. Partly as a result of its reach and scale, it is virtually impossible to provide accurate data on the number of staff, volunteers, donors and people who contribute to or benefit from the work of the Red Cross Red Crescent movement through its local branches. Such numbers would be counted in the hundreds of millions, meaning that the Red Cross Red Crescent movement is a distinctive feature of human experience in the twentieth and twenty-first centuries. This is all the more remarkable because the movement started from modest origins, with the vision of businessman turned philanthropist Henry Dunant, and the establishment of the International Committee of the Red Cross in Geneva (ICRC) in 1863.[2]

This book explores a specific moment in the history of the Red Cross Red Crescent movement when its missions and ambitions were transformed and were radically and permanently broadened at the Cannes Medical Conference of 1919. Today, people across the world associate the Red Cross Red Crescent with a wide range of humanitarian activities that greatly vary from one national context to another. Providing assistance to wounded soldiers, prisoners of war, and displaced, starving or sick civilians; assisting in national emergencies and relief operations during natural and human disasters; ambulance services, collecting blood or administering vaccinations, running hospitals, providing first aid at sporting and other events: the list of what Red Cross Red Crescent organisations do is extensive. But this was not always the Red Cross way. In fact, initially, the ambitions of the movement were limited to the battlefield. The Cannes Medical Conference was a revolutionary moment that accelerated the public health and relief turns of the Red Cross Red Crescent movement, embedding those fields of action into an expanded vision for Red Cross humanitarianism that grew over the ensuing century.[3]

The Creation and Evolution of the Red Cross Red Crescent Movement

Although the history of altruism and benevolent action started well before the establishment of the Red Cross Red Crescent movement, the type of humanitarianism developed by the Geneva-based movement has come to represent and encompass modern and contemporary notions of humanitarianism.[4] Within the Red Cross Red Crescent movement, this history has a foundational – at times quasi-messianic – narrative that both legitimised and sustained its creation. While on a business trip in 1859, Red Cross founding father Henry Dunant travelled through Solferino, the site of a major and costly battle that involved nearly a quarter of a million troops.[5] Soldiers of the Second French Empire and their ally, the Kingdom of Sardinia, fought against soldiers of the Austrian Empire. The considerable growth in the size of armies that followed the French Revolution and the Napoleonic Wars, together with the evolution of artillery and weapons systems, had major impacts on combatants' bodies. The corporeal realities of nineteenth-century warfare meant the dislocation, laceration and opening of bodies with higher casualty rates across armies.[6] It also meant more suffering in the flesh of those who waged war, and it is that suffering, the helplessness of the wounded, their lamentations and anguish that deeply moved Dunant and prompted him to act.

Visions of corpses and severely wounded men left to agonise on the battlefield are graphically described in the book that Dunant wrote about his experience, *Un Souvenir de Solférino* published three years later in 1862.[7] Dunant called for the creation of national societies to support wounded soldiers on the battlefield and that both be protected through legislation. Dunant's call was heard and a group of Genevan men – Gustave Moynier, Guillaume-Henri Dufour, Louis Appia and Théodore Maunoir – formed the International Committee of the Red Cross. A year later, in 1864, the First Geneva Convention (titled *Convention for the Amelioration of the Condition of the Wounded and Sick in Armed Forces in the Field*) was signed, with 12 states represented at a diplomatic conference convened by the Swiss government. As a result, national societies to support wounded soldiers were rapidly created throughout Western Europe, fast expanding beyond this area from the late 1860s onward.[8] The movement grew rapidly because states identified an interest in protecting their citizen-soldiers besides making war more 'humane'.

In the early days of the Red Cross Red Crescent movement, national societies trained nurses to take care of wounded soldiers and purchased equipment to assemble ambulance stations and materials necessary for the treatment of soldiers on the battlefield but also after their evacuation. Meanwhile, the ICRC continued to establish and oversee the movement, refining the Geneva Convention and obtaining more signatories, with the organisation of regular International Conferences of the Red Cross (and Red Crescent after 1868): Paris in 1867, Berlin in 1869, Geneva in 1884, Karlsruhe in 1887, Rome in 1892, Vienna in 1897, St. Petersburg in 1902, London in 1907 and Washington in 1912.[9] Those international conferences were interrupted by the First World War but managed to structure the movement with national societies closely aligned to their states' foreign policies and agendas. As conflicts erupted throughout the world between large empires, national societies were soon mobilised to fulfil their goals and assist their national armies in conflicts including, but not limited to, the Franco-Prussian war (1870–1871), the Anglo-Boer war (1899–1902) and the Russo-Japanese war (1904–1905). The work of the Red Cross was praised by armies, soldiers and civilians alike, and by the eve of the First World War, the Red Cross Red Crescent movement was already established as a quasi-universal symbol for the relief of pain and suffering on the battlefield.

The First World War, with its unprecedented toll on both soldiers and civilians, encouraged the development and expansion of the movement; the explosion of humanitarian endeavours during this period has a thorough historiography.[10] The Red Cross, perhaps paradoxically, became indispensable to states and armies in the waging of war, a force for good in the midst of Armageddon.[11] However, as the war drew closer to its end, some started to think about the future of the Red Cross movement. If the First World War was indeed the war to end all wars, then the entire movement would become redundant. There would no longer be a need to support soldiers on the battlefield if nations were not to fight anymore. But should a movement that had amassed so much support be demobilised? Could it not turn to other humanitarian activities and keep its principles alive?[12] National societies started establishing peacetime operations plans. The transition from wartime to peacetime work was on everyone's minds and the idea of *Croix-Rouge de la Paix* (Peacetime Red Cross) was discussed in several countries.[13] Admittedly, the diversification of the missions of national societies had started to occur well before the First World War. National societies such as the American, Japanese, Italian and French Red Crosses, and others too, were known to have engaged in areas of work that included public health and disaster relief, the Japanese Red Cross in particular.[14] But the movement as a whole, and in particular, under the leadership of the ICRC, did not have a consistent and global plan to organise its expansion and broaden the range of its activities.[15] To achieve this, a committee of national societies assembled and proposed the creation of a new international organisation within the Red Cross Red Crescent movement that would operate as a federation: the League of Red Cross Societies. To provide a programme of work for the future organisation, the committee called a medical conference in Cannes in 1919. This book tells the story of this conference, which ought to be understood as a watershed moment in the history of the Red Cross Red Crescent movement.

Taking place from 1 to 11 April 1919 at the *Cercle Nautique* in Cannes, in the south of France, the Cannes Medical Conference provided the *raison d'être* for the creation of the League of Red Cross Societies (the League), which was founded a month later in Paris.[16] Within the Red Cross Red Crescent movement, the League of Red Cross Societies would become the peacetime and public health-oriented equivalent to the International Committee of the Red Cross (ICRC) that focused on armed conflicts. With regard to global public health, the League can be understood as a non-government cousin or precedent to both the Health Organisation of the League of Nations created in 1920, and the World Health Organisation established in 1948. The League of Red Cross Societies was one of the first attempts at establishing a transnational humanitarian organisation whose purpose would be to work towards global improvement of health and the prevention of disease. In the aftermath of the First World War, this was identified as an urgent necessity by the initiators of the League of Red Cross Societies. To justify its foundation, they organised an international medical conference in Cannes in the spring of 1919 to discuss the world's major public health challenges, to seize the 'psychological moment' to set up such a voluntary organisation and to devise a programme of work for the new organisation. This book explores the origins, course and aftermath of the Cannes Medical Conference and its wider legacy and implications within the Red Cross Red Crescent movement. It shows that this medical conference was a landmark that helped to pivot the work of the movement across the world from wartime to peacetime work, particularly in the public health sphere. Sources that underpin this research are primarily drawn from the proceedings of the conference published by the League of Red Cross Societies, archival material available at the International Federation of Red Cross and Red Crescent Societies and the International Committee of the Red Cross's archives and libraries in Geneva, the Hoover Institution Library & Archives at Stanford University and, to a lesser extent, the National Archives and Records Administration at College Park, the archives of the French Foreign Office at La Courneuve, and the *Bibliothèque Nationale de France*, in Paris.

The Cannes Medical Conference and the League of Red Cross Societies

Today, in Geneva, there exists an international organisation called the International Federation of Red Cross and Red Crescent Societies (IFRC), a humanitarian organisation that counts 191 member national Red Cross Red Crescent societies.[17] The IFRC, which evolved throughout the tumultuous twentieth century and into the twenty-first century, was initially known as the League of Red Cross Societies. It was founded on 5 May 1919 in Paris by the American, British, Italian, Japanese and French Red Cross national societies, with the ambition to alleviate human suffering in peacetime and improve global public health.[18] The origins of this organisation can be traced to one man, an eminent supporter of his, and a specific historical moment. The man was Henry Pomeroy Davison, a banker with J. P. Morgan who became Chairman of the American Red Cross War Council; the eminent supporter was Woodrow Wilson, the President of the United States of America from 1913 to 1921 and the Honorary President of the American Red Cross; and the moment was the 'end' of the First World War, which radically transformed the international geopolitical landscape. Through an analysis of Davison's correspondence with Wilson, his office, and key players in the American Red Cross and the banking worlds, historians Melanie Oppenheimer and Carolyn Collins have documented how the idea for the League of Red Cross Societies germinated in the United States of America at the end of 1918 before being implemented by Davison throughout 1919 and 1920.[19]

This book seeks to contribute to and contextualise the 'origin story' of the League by investigating its foundational moment: the Cannes Medical Conference. The conference was organised by the Committee of Red Cross Societies, a self-styled assemblage of the five Red Cross national societies of the United States, the United Kingdom, France, Japan and Italy, which was led by Henry P. Davison and announced to the press in February 1919 at a glamorous public dinner in Paris.[20] The national societies that formed this Committee would later become the founding members of the League of Red Cross Societies, but before this, a number of steps needed to be taken to both justify and gain broad support for the project. What would a global health organisation within the Red Cross Red Crescent movement look like? Was it necessary? How would it work, and what would be the key priorities? Those questions needed to be answered and a roadmap established before the League of Red Cross Societies could be created. The Cannes Medical Conference was the opportunity to do just that.

Of course, the Cannes Medical Conference, both as a method and as an outcome, did not happen in a vacuum. Nevertheless, the dominance of the

First World War context should not overshadow major trends and shifts that emerged in the previous century. Mark Mazower has written about the 'era of transnationalism' that preceded the First World War and that continued after it, an era in which he convincingly claims that science acted as a 'unifier'.[21] International expertise was increasingly being drawn upon to resolve major global issues, and to standardise measurements such as time, sizes and distances, for example. Drawing on 'expert knowledge' and the 'rise of networks of experts' became a feature of this period, in national, imperial and international frameworks alike.[22] In this context of an 'international turn' 'in the age of nationalism' and apex of empire explored by Glenda Sluga[23] – frameworks that surprisingly were not antithetical but managed to work hand in hand – the Cannes Medical Conference arises as one of many landmarks that paved the way for the internationalisation of global responses to public health challenges.[24]

This book investigates what it demonstrates to be the missing link in the transformation and evolution of the world's largest humanitarian network. The Cannes Medical Conference enabled a major paradigm shift that expanded the work of the whole Red Cross Red Crescent movement from wartime work to peacetime work, including public health, disaster management work and relief. The Conference was the most decisive step in creating the League of Red Cross Societies, which attempted to oversee and support the coordination of Red Cross Red Crescent activity across the globe. Public health and humanitarianism are both major fields of research, as is the study of the Red Cross Red Crescent movement specifically. Despite this, however, no study to date has analysed the Cannes Medical Conference and its lasting impacts on the Red Cross movement.[25] This book aims to redress this situation, contributing to the historiography of these fields of research.

It is divided into five chapters. Chapter 1 places the Cannes Medical Conference within the evolution of the Red Cross Red Crescent movement. It analyses the tectonic changes at play in the movement at a time when national societies sought to expand the scope of their activities while navigating a somewhat cautious and at times reluctant ICRC. Chapter 2 provides background to the Cannes Medical Conference, reviewing medical conferences that preceded it and where they fell short. Until Cannes, there had been no successful attempts at creating a truly international organisation that would make recommendations and take action on the issue of global public health. Chapter 3 contextualises the conference within what some have called the 'Wilsonian moment': a time that saw a reconfiguration of the world order. It posits that the Cannes Medical Conference and the subsequent creation of the League of Red Cross Societies were not a revolution for the Red Cross movement, but an evolution, an expansion in a global context of post-war health emergency. Chapter 4 focuses on the enthusiasm of the conference delegates for the founding of a global health organisation, and it investigates the differences in visions that conference delegates and Davison had over the shape and functions of the organisation that they were hoping would be born from Cannes. The last and final chapter, Chapter 5, considers how the Cannes Medical Conference defined the missions of the League of Red Cross Societies and set it up to be the Red Cross's peacetime body, with a focus on public health prevention, training for and coordination of Red Cross activity across the world.

On the whole, this book is an attempt to conceptualise the Cannes Medical Conference as both a point of arrival for the Red Cross Red Crescent movement and a new beginning. While a significant number of national societies had started to work in the public health field at home prior to the First World War, until the Cannes Medical Conference there had been no serious attempt within the movement to coordinate such action at a global level and to make this area of work a central feature of the movement that every national society should be encouraged to pursue. In achieving this by giving birth to the League of Red Cross Societies, the Cannes Medical Conference is a landmark moment in the history of the Red Cross Red Crescent movement and global public health.

Notes

1 This book uses the terminology 'Red Cross Red Crescent movement' but acknowledges that in the period under investigation the movement was largely – but certainly not exclusively – Western-centric and operating within an imperial and economically liberal framework, with Christian values widespread among the leadership of the ICRC and that of dominant Western national societies. However, the declining Ottoman Empire was among the earliest to form a Red Crescent society in the Muslim world (1869), which it heavily mobilised during the First World War. The Red Crescent symbol, though used by the Ottomans (and then by the Turks) and the Egyptians, was only formally approved by the movement in 1929 as an official symbol. For more information on the Red Crescent before, during and shortly after the First World War, see the content and useful bibliography in Esther Möller, 'Red Crescent (Hilal-i Ahmer)', in: *1914–1918-online. International Encyclopedia of the First World War*, edited by Ute Daniel, Peter Gatrell, Oliver Janz, Heather Jones, Jennifer Keene, Alan Kramer, and Bill Nasson (Berlin: issued by Freie Universität Berlin, 2019).

2 Unless otherwise indicated, historical developments presented in this introduction are discussed in: Clyde E. Buckingham, *For humanity's Sake: the Story of the Early Development of the League of Red Cross Societies* (Washington: Public Affairs Press, 1964); John F. Hutchinson, *Champions of Charity: War and the Rise of the Red* (Boulder: Westview Press, 1996); Caroline Moorehead, *Dunant's Dream: War, Switzerland, and the History of the Red Cross* (New York: Carroll & Graf Publisher, 1999) and Irène Herrmann, *L'humanitaire en questions: réflexions autour de l'histoire du Comité international de la Croix-Rouge* (Paris: Les Éditions du Cerf, 2018).

3 Given that the focus of this book is the Cannes Medical Conference, it is the public health aspect of the League of Red Cross Societies' program of work that this book considers, rather than relief operations.
4 Michael Barnett, *Empire of Humanity: A History of Humanitarianism* (Ithaca: Cornell University Press, 2011), 1–18.
5 'Biography of Henry Dunant' in the Henri Dunant (sic) files, A0905/2, box R510385965, IFRC archives, Geneva.
6 Stéphane Audoin-Rouzeau, *Combattre: une anthropologie historique de la guerre moderne, XIXe-XXIe siècle* (Paris: Seuil, 2008), 239–315.
7 Henry Dunant, *Un Souvenir de Solférino* (Genève: Imprimerie Jules-Guillaume Fick, 1862).
8 'Dates of Foundation of National Societies from 1863 to 1963', *International Review of the Red Cross*, no. 54 (1965): 499–502.
9 The full list is available on the ICRC's website: https://www.icrc.org/en/doc/resources/documents/misc/57jnvs.htm [accessed 5 June 2024].
10 A summary of this historiography is provided in Cédric Cotter, 'Red Cross' in *1914–1918-online. International Encyclopedia of the First World War*, eds. Ute Daniel, Peter Gatrell, Oliver Janz, Heather Jones, Jennifer Keene, Alan Kramer, and Bill Nasson (Berlin: issued by Freie Universität Berlin, 2018. DOI: 10.15463/ie1418.11237 [Accessed 24 October 2024]. See also *Humanitarianism and the Greater War 1914–24*, eds. Elisabeth Piller and Neville Wylie, (Manchester: Manchester University Press, 2023).
11 Heather Jones, 'International or transnational? Humanitarian action during the First World War', *European Review of History: Revue Européenne d'histoire*, 16, no. 5 (2009): 697–713.
12 *Proceedings of the Medical Conference held at the Invitation of the Committee of Red Cross Societies, Cannes, France, April 1 to 11, 1919* (Geneva: League of Red Cross Societies, 1919), 18 and 23.
13 There is a fascinating file available at the ICRC's archives with clippings from news articles in which different national societies (American, French, British, German, Swiss, Danish) and their representatives discuss their plans for the future, and the type of peacetime work they intend to undertake. The ICRC was following these developments closely. See CR 29-01 'Croix-Rouge de la Paix. Coupures', ICRC archives, Geneva.
14 Romain Fathi and Melanie Oppenheimer, 'The Shôken Fund and the evolution of the Red Cross movement', *European Review of History: Revue Européenne d'histoire* 30, no. 5 (2023): 813–816.
15 'Conférence des Croix-Rouges alliées à Genève', *Journal de Genève*, 13 February 1919.
16 Despite its key role in the creation of the League of Red Cross Societies and its contribution to shifting the work of the Red Cross movement, scholarship on the conference itself is scant. It includes: *La Conférence Médicale de Cannes*, ed. Roger Durand (Genève: Société Henry Dunant, 1994); Clyde E. Buckingham, *For Humanity's Sake*, 66–75; Melanie Oppenheimer, '"A golden moment?": The League of Red Cross Societies, the League of Nations and contested spaces of internationalism and humanitarianism, 1919–1922', in *League of Nations: Histories, Legacies and Impact*, eds. Joy Damousi and Patricia O'Brien (Melbourne: Melbourne University Press, 2018), 17–19 and Norman Howard-Jones, *International Public Health Between the Two World Wars. The Organisational Problems* (Geneva: World Health Organisation, 1978), 9–13.
17 https://www.ifrc.org/national-societies [Accessed 10 October 2024].

INTRODUCTION

18 The official name of the organisation evolved from the League of Red Cross Societies in 1919 to the League of Red Cross and Red Crescent Societies in 1983, and then to the International Federation of Red Cross and Red Crescent Societies in 1991, a name it has kept ever since.
19 Melanie Oppenheimer and Carolyn Collins, *Henry Pomeroy Davison 1867–1922* (Geneva: Société Henry Dunant & International Federation of Red Cross and Red Crescent Societies, 2019), 47–63. Henry Pomeroy Davison was born in Troy, Pennsylvania, USA in 1867 and passed away in 1922. His involvement with the Red Cross has been documented in the aforementioned book and further information on his life can be accessed in: Thomas W. Lamont, *Henry P. Davison: the Record of a Useful Life* (New York: Harper, 1933); *Henry Pomeroy Davison: a Memorial* (New York: Bankers Trust Company, 1922) and *The Henry P. Davison Scholarships* (New York: Select printing co., 1927).
20 'Croix-Rouge. Un programme d'actions des Croix-Rouge', *Le Gaulois*, 22 February 1919. These five national societies developed close relationships throughout the war with an impressive track record of collaboration.
21 Mark Mazower, *Governing the World. The History of an Idea, 1815 to the Present* (New York: Penguin Books, 2012), 94–115.
22 *Shaping the Transnational Sphere: Experts, Networks, and Issues from the 1840s to the 1930s*, eds. Davide Rodogno, Bernhard Struck and Jakob Vogel (New York: Berghahn, 2015), 1.
23 Glenda Sluga, *Internationalism in the Age of Nationalism* (Philadelphia: University of Pennsylvania Press, 2013), 11–44.
24 Other such landmarks in a nineteenth century context are briefly outlined in Chapter II of this book. For those landmarks that followed the First World War, please refer to *International Health Organisations and Movements, 1918–1939*, ed. Paul Weindling (Cambridge: Cambridge University Press, 1995).
25 An exception exists, in French. Titled *La conférence médicale de Cannes*, this edited volume was published in 1994 by the Société Henry Dunant. Although the book has a focus on the city of Cannes and its history and serves commemorative purposes, two chapters in particular discuss the Cannes Medical Conference in relation to the evolution of the Red Cross movement: Roger Durand, 'La Conférence médicale, ses participants et le *Bulletin de la Ligue des Sociétés de la Croix-Rouge*' and Jean Guillermand, 'La Croix-Rouge américaine et le corps médical français'.

Chapter 1

TECTONIC SHIFTS IN THE RED CROSS RED CRESCENT MOVEMENT

Before Cannes, the leading body of the Red Cross Red Crescent movement was the International Committee of the Red Cross (ICRC) based in Geneva. Established in 1863, the ICRC was primarily responsible for alleviating human suffering during times of war and regulating conflicts through the development of international humanitarian law. After the First World War, the ICRC did not wish to be altered too radically, either in terms of structure or in terms of mission. The idea that a new international Red Cross organisation would emerge, or that this organisation would be in competition with the ICRC, surprised and troubled its leadership. Even if what would later be called the League of Red Cross Societies was to operate in a totally different landscape – that of peacetime, in the fields of public health and relief – the process of its creation, which includes the Cannes Medical Conference, was a challenging experience for the ICRC. This chapter considers how Henry P. Davison and representatives of the five national societies that he had assembled within a Committee of Red Cross Societies engaged with the ICRC in their attempt to transform the movement. In other words, this chapter contextualises the Cannes Medical Conference within a greater, longer and more complex process of negotiation between different visions for the future of the movement because it was not only about public health but also about the politics, structures and governance of the movement. This period of fast-paced negotiations enables the conceptualisation of the Cannes Medical Conference as a lens through which to observe the tectonic changes at play in the Red Cross Red Crescent movement at a time when national societies sought to expand the scope of their activities navigating a somewhat cautious and at times reluctant ICRC.

Henry Pomeroy Davison: A Man in a Hurry

Henry Pomeroy Davison was born in Troy, Pennsylvania, in 1867, where after receiving an education he started to work at his uncle's bank in 1887.[1] Over the following 20 years, he would climb the banking ladder, moving from one appointment to the next until he joined one of the world's most respected banks: J.P. Morgan & Co. By the outbreak of the First World War, Henry P. Davison had become a prominent figure within the American world of banking. In May 1917, a month after the United States entered the First World War, he was approached by President Woodrow Wilson to become the Chairman of the War Council of the American Red Cross. 'Despite [his] wariness of Republicans and Wall Street men', Wilson, who also held the title of Honorary President of the American Red Cross, needed someone who could be successful in raising large sums of money to support the wartime activities of the national society.[2] Davison obliged, and Wilson's bet proved far-sighted. By the 1918 Armistice, the coffers of the American Red Cross were overflowing, radically altering the scale and scope of the national society's operations and ensuring its hegemonic position within the movement.[3] As the war drew to an end, Davison started to think about how the Red Cross could remain a force for good in peacetime. He presented Wilson with his early ideas for a global, peacetime, public health Red Cross, for which a programme of work was to be established at the Cannes Medical Conference.

Before delegates assembled at Cannes in April 1919, Davison did much preliminary work to obtain support from national societies of wartime allied countries for his project of the peacetime Red Cross.[4] He also tried to secure the support of the ICRC itself, seeking an official mandate for the people he had assembled to establish a plan for the post-war Red Cross under the auspices of the ICRC. From the start, this *modus operandi* was greeted with caution by the ICRC. The Red Cross movement was neutral (at least in principle), and the emergence of a new organisation within the Red Cross movement that was supported by a specific group of wartime allied national societies could be seen as a partisan move, departing from tradition. What about those who were defeated during the war? Were their Red Cross national societies going to be excluded from the great battle for health? Besides such legitimate questions, the ICRC was also concerned that it would lose its primary position within the movement. If war was over and the ICRC was a wartime or war-related institution, what was it going to become?

The ICRC was, of course, not impervious to public health and relief developments that had occurred within some national societies prior to and during the First World War. In fact, as early as November 1918, ICRC leadership had written to all national societies to ask about their peacetime plans and the programmes of work they may want to undertake after the signing of the Peace, suspected to be only a few months away.[5] This was happening somewhat concomitantly to Davison's great push for a League of Red Cross Societies, as his first meeting with President Wilson to discuss such an organisation was held in early December 1918, with his ideas germinating during his 1918 European tours earlier in the year. The ICRC was aware that the missions of the Red Cross Red Crescent movement, and its own missions, were bound to evolve once peace treaties were signed.[6] As opposed to Davison, however, the ICRC wanted to take time to deliberate on the movement's future by entering into a dialogue about such prospects with *all* national societies at the forthcoming 10th International Conference of the Red Cross. Delayed because of the war, the ICRC wished that this International Conference be held within 30 days of peace treaties being concluded. As it happened, the last treaty of the Paris Peace Conference was not signed until 10 August 1920, at Sèvres. Furthermore, the ICRC did not fully anticipate the determination of the French, the Belgian and the British Red Crosses not to sit at the same table as German Red Cross representatives, at least not for another year or two, further delaying the next International Conference of the Red Cross.[7] What it was perhaps most unaware of, in the last days of 1918, was that its position within the movement was about to be shaken by a group of five national societies led by Henry Pomeroy Davison. In the early days of 1919, the ICRC faced a number of challenges: its finances were in decline, it was not clear when the next International Conference of the Red Cross would take place, the role and missions of the Red Cross Red Crescent national societies themselves needed rethinking, all the while the ICRC's work with prisoners of war remained immense.

For Davison, there was no time to waste. The Red Cross needed to take its public health turn now: it could not wait for an International Conference of the Red Cross, the timing of which was unknown, even if this meant that former enemies would not, initially, be included as part of this transformation. After the Armistice, Davison's role within the American Red Cross required him to envision a future for the movement in peacetime at the national level; but his thinking did not limit itself to the American Red Cross. Instead, he wanted the Red Cross Red Crescent movement as a whole to seize peacetime as an opportunity to transform itself, remain relevant, and do good in the space of public health and relief. Melanie Oppenheimer and Carolyn Collins have established a chronology that testifies to Davison's velocity in transforming a vision for the future of the Red Cross movement into a reality. He first met with President Wilson on 2 December 1918 to discuss this 'remote possibility' and boarded a ship to Europe within a fortnight to garner support for his idea of an expanded peacetime Red Cross with a focus on public health. By 1 February 1919, Davison announced the formation of the Committee of Red Cross Societies that included the United States, the United Kingdom, Italy, France and Japan's national societies.[8] On 21 February, the plans of the Committee were made public in Paris.[9] These were the steps that preceded the Cannes Conference Medical and the foundation of the League of Red Cross Societies itself. The pace of Davison's actions is remarkable. While this was happening, the ICRC closely watched the developments. Initially, Davison was hoping that his vision, supported by others, could be realised by the ICRC itself. It soon became evident, however, that the ICRC would not and could not achieve what the Committee of Red Cross Societies headed by Davison had in mind.

After announcing the formation of a Committee of Red Cross Societies, Davison wasted no time in getting the work of the Committee underway. On 2 February 1919, he assembled representatives of the five national societies that composed the Committee to prepare a collective response to the ICRC's 27 November 1918 circular that asked all national societies to advise on their peacetime programme of work and how they wished for the movement to evolve in that space in the aftermath of the conflict.[10] This was a time when Davison thought that he could still transform the ICRC, encouraging it to carry out the great American project of an expanded, federated and public health-oriented Red Cross movement, well supported by Japan, Italy and the United Kingdom, and slightly less so by the French who sent an observer rather than a delegate to the meeting.[11] Davison's vision was that the 'international Red Cross located at Geneva w[ould] enlarge its scope and influence and w[ould] become the medium of transmission of knowledge and the instrument coordinating the activities and resources of Red Cross organisations'.[12] Essentially, Davison hoped that the ICRC would internationalise and open up its recruitment process, have a more democratic and federalist structure, and turn to peacetime and relief work. This did not happen, and so he pressed ahead to create an organisation that would do all these things. The establishment of the League of Red Cross Societies on 5 May 1919 was not a fait accompli, Davison had hoped that the ICRC would change from the inside.

ICRC minutes shed light on Davison's vision and how it was perceived by members of the ICRC. Davison's initial intention was not to create an entirely new organisation within the movement.[13] This was clear to ICRC members who understood that Davison wanted to meet with them to suggest modifications to the ICRC with Wilson's direct support.[14] Such modifications included a Red Cross with a leadership more representative of national societies – the ICRC was exclusively Genevan – and considerably expanded peacetime missions for the movement. There was ongoing and frequent communication between Davison and the ICRC in the first half of 1919. These exchanges were often facilitated by William Rappard, a Harvard University graduate and Swiss diplomat who acted as a benevolent intermediary, given his linguistic and cross-cultural abilities.[15] Exchanges between Davison and the ICRC climaxed mid-February when Davison, with representatives of the five national societies, met with the ICRC for three consecutive days. Gustave Ador and nine other members of the ICRC were in attendance, facing Davison and six representatives of the United States, the United Kingdom, Italy, Japan and France's Red Cross national societies, with another two American delegates joining from day two. This was an important moment in the history of the Red Cross. One can only wonder what would have happened to the movement had the ICRC accepted the Committee's proposal.

The Attempt to Bring the ICRC on Board

From 12 to 14 February 1919, Davison and representatives of the Committee of Red Cross Societies met with ICRC members in Geneva. From the very beginning of the three-day event, it was clear that the ICRC would be hard to change. In his opening statement, ICRC President *ad interim* Edouard Naville explained: 'A few among you may not be exactly informed about the character of the International Committee and its origin, which you will allow me to remind you of in a few words'.[16] Given those in attendance at the meeting, the comment was likely pointed at Davison and members of the American delegation. Naville continued: 'La Croix-Rouge est une institution de guerre. Elle a été créée en vue de la guerre' ('the Red Cross is a war-related institution. It has been created in anticipation for war'). He explained that this very purpose compelled the ICRC to be neutral, implying that Davison's enterprise went against the very fundamentals of the ICRC because it represented a select group of First World War allies. The neutrality of the ICRC, according to Naville, was grounded in Swiss neutrality, reinforcing its global credibility and it was, purportedly, totally devoid of political ambitions, here hinting at Davison's connection to the Wilsonian project. Naville continued his preamble by linking the ICRC's successes during the First World War to this very neutrality. If the message was not clear enough, the President *ad interim* declared that 'complete neutrality and absolute independence' were the most important characteristics for ICRC success.

After this long creeping barrage of considerations, Naville explained that the ICRC was aware that the Red Cross was entering into a new era and that, to that effect, it had started consulting national societies through its 27 November 1918 circular. He acknowledged that the ICRC, as a whole, was enthusiastic about the peacetime plan presented by Davison and the five national societies, and fully supportive of the peacetime programme of work they were advocating for. However, for the ICRC, such a programme ought to be discussed once all peace treaties have been signed, with all national societies part of the conversation. The Allies – a limited albeit powerful group – could not be solely responsible for the peacetime programme of the Red Cross movement. Expressing the views of ICRC members, Naville explained that they might be willing to open up membership to non-Geneva citizens and change both its missions and its motto from *Inter Arma Caritas* to *Post Arma Caritas*. These were far from insignificant concessions for the ICRC, but not quite what the Americans and Davison had in mind.

In his response to Naville and ICRC members, Davison acknowledged the importance of neutrality, yet he antithetically suggested that 'the coordination of Red Cross societies may be a starting point for the League of Nations'.[17] This was not received positively by ICRC representatives, as they did not wish to become subordinated to a large international government organisation or to be absorbed into what many perceived to be a Wilsonian – and therefore American – project. This did not align with their idea of independence and neutrality. Little did they know that the United States would never join the League of Nations.

Although Davison acknowledged that the ICRC ought to lead its own transformation, he suggested that it should accept the plan formulated ten days prior by the five national societies of his Committee. That plan, which he detailed to Naville and ICRC representatives, was essentially the League of Red Cross Societies in embryo form and included the organisation of a conference of medical experts to establish a programme of activities sanctioned by medical professionals. In his characteristically brash American style, Davison concluded: 'nowadays, nothing is impossible anymore'.[18] The British delegate, Sir Arthur Lawley, expressed his national society's full support of Davison's plan for the future of the Red Cross Red Crescent movement, as did the Japanese and Italian representatives; the French were more reserved. The presentation of everyone's position concluded the first day of the proceedings.

Ever the diplomat, at least in public, Gustave Ador – both former and future ICRC President but then President of the Swiss Federation in Bern – spoke on the second day of the gathering and opened his address by stating that there was a 'perfect concordance of views' between the plan formulated by the five national societies and the ICRC's vision for the directions the movement should take.[19] He proposed that the ICRC double down on its 27 November 1918 circular and draft a new one to both confirm that the Red Cross movement would transition to peacetime work and to invite national societies to propose their plans for such a transformation. These would then be discussed at an International Conference of the Red Cross to be organised after the signing of the peace treaties. Ador suggested that for now, however, this new Red Cross peacetime programme should deal with the immediate consequences of war such as disabilities, infant mortality and diseases, which were more closely aligned with the traditional role of the Red Cross. Ador's statement revealed the ICRC's reluctance to see the Red Cross Red Crescent movement move too far away from war-related missions.

Davison indicated that he was supportive of the ICRC's plan and timeline, but inferred that it was too limited in terms of scope. Davison wished for the ICRC to coordinate global public health action based on the recommendation of health experts. Ador argued that it would be best for such expert views to be gathered *after* the International Conference of the Red Cross, rather than before. This is where Ador's and Davison's visions explicitly diverged. Davison thought that it would be best to take a health programme to the next International Conference of the Red Cross, rather than to have experts come up with one after the conference based on a plurality of submissions made by national societies. Davison thought that if a programme was ready ahead of the conference, attendees could adopt the programme and get national societies to start its implementation immediately. For Davison, time was of the essence, now was the moment to act.[20] Davison reinforced his point and explained that one of the reasons why he wanted a conference of experts to be assembled prior to the next International Conference of the Red Cross was that it would result in a precise, detailed programme, as opposed to '75', a number he used hyperbolically.[21] For him, asking the views of every national society on a peacetime programme for the Red Cross would lead to disagreement, delay and potentially, inertia. Whether Davison's intuition was correct or not, this would undeniably delay the Red Cross's public health turn, making it slower to arrive and implement. This may have been Ador's aim. Beyond the principles it evoked, such as neutrality, independence and consensus, it is clear that the ICRC was playing for time.

Although in disagreement, Ador asked Davison to explain precisely how he wanted to proceed. Davison obliged by listing step by step how he envisioned the medical conference would be convened and to what ends.[22] What he laid out before Ador became the Cannes Medical Conference. By mid-February, Davison hoped that the ICRC would take up, or at least endorse his plan of a medical conference, but no such support was forthcoming. In the end, he made it happen without the ICRC, drawing on his ample resources to do so.[23] After Davison had laid out how the medical conference would be organised and the purposes it would serve, Naville asked him if the Central Powers would be invited to the conference. Davison replied that they would not – because of British and French opposition in particular – but that they could be kept informed by a member of the ICRC who would attend the medical conference. Des Gouttes, the ICRC's Secretary, commented that Davison's conference could not be recognised by the ICRC or considered as an official commission within the movement if it were to be attended by five Allied national societies only. The exclusion of former enemies went against the movement's principles.

The views of Davison could not be reconciled with those of the ICRC. In a final attempt to get the ICRC on the side, Davison emphasised his political connections. He suggested that Ador accompany him to Paris to meet with the British, French and Italian Prime ministers, David Lloyd George, Georges Clemenceau and Vittorio Orlando, and the representative of the US's President, Edward M. House, so that he could announce a new plan for the international Red Cross at a dinner for the Press. Ador, then President of the Swiss Confederation, politely replied that he could not commit as he may be sent to Paris as a political representative and could not deal with both Swiss and Red Cross matters at once. Unfazed, Davison ended up organising the dinner on 21 February, to which the ICRC sent representatives.[24] Even the ICRC acknowledged that the dinner for the Press was a resounding success.[25]

The outcome of the three-day meeting was that the work of Davison and the representatives of the five national societies would not be officially endorsed or acknowledged by the ICRC because of the neutrality issue, and disagreement on process and timing. However, the ICRC supported the continuation of the work of the five national societies and agreed that public health and relief would become major fields of activity for the Red Cross in the post-war world. Overall, ICRC minutes reveal that 'M. Davison in no way wishes to eliminate Geneva and the International Committee'.[26] But they also reveal that the Committee was in awe of Davison's great vision for the Red Cross movement, a vision that seemed to some far too large and ambitious. They recognised that Davison's aim was for the ICRC to take up this new programme of work in a modified, enlarged organisation that was to be the 'centre of coordinated efforts' for the movement.[27] This is not how the ICRC viewed itself, nor did it have the means to carry out such work. Rightly or wrongly, Ador feared that the Americans wanted to radically transform the Red Cross Red Crescent movement to place it under the League of Nations.[28] This reluctance was shared by the French in particular, who were the most cautious of Davison's vision, fearing American imperialism and 'Anglo-Saxon' hegemony over the movement.[29] The Vice President of the French Red Cross, Vice Amiral Touchard, however, told a member of the ICRC that France had to follow the Americans, 'even without enthusiasm'.[30] That is because the French had far more pressing issues to resolve at Versailles with regard to Germany's future and they were keen to receive American support in exchange for easily granted concessions, such as Wilson's vision for a League of Nations and that of an expanded Red Cross.[31]

The ICRC resolved to 'appear very friendly' towards the Americans, all the while 'limiting the action of Red Crosses to the domain that belongs to them, that is the victims of war, without encroaching on the field of activity of independent organisations such as charities for children, labour legislation, venereal diseases'.[32] In other words, the ICRC was not interested in taking up Davison's full programme of work, although it recognised that its activities and that of Red Cross Red Crescent national societies would evolve in peacetime. With millions of prisoners of war (POWs) to deal with and many lingering war-related issues, the ICRC was already overstretched, in terms of resources in particular.[33] At that time, the ICRC was an emergency institution, one forced to focus on what needed to be done now rather than developing plans for a more distant future. Ultimately, it was decided to turn once again to national societies to ask what they wanted to do in peacetime. And so, for now, 'before M. Davison and his colleagues, the International Committee will present itself as determined to orient the action of Red Cross societies toward peacetime work, while prioritising war-derived work, qualified nursing, relief for the wounded, and tuberculosis'.[34]

Between the end of this three-day gathering and the opening of the Cannes Medical Conference on 1 April, the ICRC followed Davison's activities closely. The ICRC could not stop the initiative of the five national societies and so it resolved to appear supportive of it while somewhat keeping its distance. Now that Davison's medical conference was going to happen, it was a better strategy to attend the conference than to ignore it. From 5 April 1919, some sessions of the Cannes Medical Conference were attended by Edouard Naville, and Miss Renée-Marguerite Cramer, another ICRC member. When he first spoke at the Cannes Medical Conference, Naville explained that he was not attending as an official delegate of the ICRC, which he felt would negatively impact its neutral position. When discussing the potential future peacetime Red Cross organisation in relation to the movement, and in particular, the transition to peacetime work and public health, Naville explained that present circumstances at a time when peace treaties were not signed made it 'impossible' for the ICRC to unite all Red Cross national societies around a peacetime programme. This was partly because some national societies (the Belgian, British and French Red Crosses) categorically refused to sit at a table where the national societies of their enemies would be represented as well.[35] Davison immediately answered Naville by explaining that this is precisely why the new Committee of Red Cross Societies – the body that would create the League of Red Cross Societies a month later – had been formed: to circumvent that issue and start peacetime work now, given the 'urgent necessity of beginning work on an international scale at once'.[36] For Davison, something was better than nothing. Davison was a pragmatist.

Although he hoped that ultimately all nations would be incorporated into the new organisation, through both existing Red Cross national societies and those that would be created in the years to come, he knew that this would need to wait. In the interim, the support of the key allies who had won the war was essential to kick-start the organisation, even if it meant that this group would initially exclude former foes. In response to Naville, however, Davison declared that it was the desire of the Committee of Red Cross Societies to 'work anywhere and at all times in the fullest co-operation with the International Red Cross'.[37]

Given the ICRC's stand on neutrality as the central tenet of its action, it is understandable that it could not take on a mission that would exclude some Red Cross national societies. This, however, did not mean that members of the ICRC were in disagreement with Davison's idea. In fact, Naville was quite supportive of what he referred to as *la Croix-Rouge de la Paix*, but the centrality of the American Red Cross within the yet-to-be-born organisation, together with a complete change of structure and programme of work, was too much to ask from the ICRC.[38] It was neither equipped – in terms of staff, material, resources and organisational structure – nor willing to become the Red Cross for Peace given that the whole movement to date had been designed to alleviate wartime suffering.

Both before and after the Cannes Medical Conference, Davison liaised with ICRC representatives to enquire as to whether the organisation he envisioned could be supported by or amalgamated with the ICRC, but to no avail. Despite this setback, as noted by historian Roger Durand, with Cannes 'Davison dispose de la caution des spécialistes et du monde croix-rouge qui lui permet de négocier en position de force' (Davison was backed by specialists and the Red Cross world which enabled him to negotiate from a position of strength).[39] The ICRC's reluctance to accept the proposal from which the League of Red Cross Societies would emerge was not an ideological one. Rather, it was an acknowledgement that the ICRC was not the right tool to achieve the plan of the Committee of Red Cross Societies at that time, that the principle of neutrality was paramount to ICRC action, and that perhaps most importantly, a federated model for the Red Cross was not supported in Geneva. Nevertheless, given the rising interest in public health among Red Cross national societies (that of Switzerland included) and the challenge posed by the new League of Red Cross Societies after its creation on 5 May 1919, the ICRC soon changed tack and started to include peacetime work and public health among its missions within a few months of the League's creation.[40] With the founding of the League, the public health genie was finally and decisively out of the bottle for the Red Cross Red Crescent movement, with the hands of its historic and *primus inter pares* committee, the ICRC – if not forced – heavily influenced by Davison and his Committee of Red Cross Societies. The Cannes Medical Conference is the transitional moment that enabled the transformation of an idea, of a vision, into a programme of work embodied in an institution provided with financial resources to action it.

Notes

1 Unless indicated otherwise, biographical information on Henry P. Davison come from: Oppenheimer and Collins, *Henry Pomeroy Davison 1867–1922*.
2 Ibid., 35. See also Melanie Oppenheimer, '"A golden moment?" [...]', 11–16. For Davison's work beyond the Red Cross, in finance, see: Richard A. Naclerio, 'The Emissary: Henry P. Davison' In *The Federal Reserve and Its Founders: Money, Politics and Power* (Newcastle upon Tyne: Agenda Publishing, 2018), 97–114.
3 Julia Irwin, *Making the World Safe. The American Red Cross and a Nation's Humanitarian Awakening* (Oxford: Oxford University Press, 2013), 74–78.
4 Romain Fathi, 'Sovereignty, Democracy and Neutrality: French Foreign Policy and the National-Patriotic Humanitarianism of the French Red Cross, 1919–1928', *Contemporary European History* 32, no. 2 (2021): 308–309.
5 ICRC circular, 'La mission du comité international de la Croix-Rouge pendant et après la guerre', 27 November 1918. See Irène Herrmann, 'Humanitaire et paix: une équation impossible?' in *Action humanitaire et quête de la Paix* (Genève: Fondation Gustave Ador & Georg Editeur, 2018): 35–36.
6 Ibid.
7 Fathi, 'Sovereignty, Democracy and Neutrality [...]', 310–312.
8 Oppenheimer and Collins, *Henry Pomeroy Davison 1867–1922*, 88–89.
9 'Croix-Rouge. Un programme d'action des Croix-Rouges', *Le Gaulois*, 22 February 1919.
10 Davison to ICRC, 4 February 1919 in file 'Conférence de Genève Février 1919', CR 30-1, ICRC archives, Geneva. Amiral Touchard (Vice President, French Red Cross) explained the same to Edouard Naville (ICRC President *ad interim*) in a letter dated 6 February 1919 located in the same file.
11 This is covered in Oppenheimer and Collins, *Henry Pomeroy Davison 1867–1922*, 50–55. See also Irène Herrmann, 'Décrypter la concurrence humanitaire: le conflit entre Croix-Rouge(s) après 1918', *Relations internationales* 3, no. 151 (2012): 91–102 and Roger Durand, *'La Conférence Médicale de Cannes, ses participants et le Bulletin de la Ligue des Sociétés de la Croix-Rouge'*, 58.
12 Davison to ICRC, 6 February 1919 in file 'Conférence de Genève Février 1919', CR 30-1, ICRC, Geneva.
13 Oppenheimer and Collins, *Henry Pomeroy Davison 1867–1922*, 51; Melanie Oppenheimer, '"A golden moment?" [...]', 15–16.
14 2 January 1919 entry in *Comité International de la Croix-Rouge. Agence des prisonniers de guerre*, volume 2, box A PV A AIPG 1–2, ICRC archives, Geneva, henceforth referred to as ICRC minutes.
15 Born in New York of Swiss parents, Rappard contributed a great deal to the League of Nations' Secretariat and was for a time on the ICRC committee, a bridge between the American and Swiss worlds. He became involved with numerous organisations throughout his life, such as the International Labour Organisation and the UN

as Swiss representative. In 1919–1920 Rappard was also Secretary General of the League of Red Cross Societies. See Sandrine Kott and Grégoire Carasso, 'The making of International Geneva', *SwissInfo*, 16 July 2018; Richard M. Ebeling, 'William E. Rappard: An International Man in an Age of Nationalism', *The Freeman: Ideas on Liberty or Ideas on Liberty* 50, no. 1 (2000).

16 Unless otherwise indicated, the synthesis of information provided in the following paragraphs originates from: *Procès verbaux entrevue des Croix-Rouges alliées et du Comité International à Genève*, 12 February 1919, in file 'Hors Inventaire' CR 30, ICRC, Geneva.
17 Ibid.
18 Ibid.
19 *Procès verbaux entrevue des Croix-Rouges alliées et du Comité International à Genève*, 13 February 1919 in file 'Hors Inventaire' CR 30, ICRC archives, Geneva. For Ador's later private views on Davison's project and the League of Red Cross Societies more generally, see the letters he sent to his daughter and son-in-law in *Lettres à Germaine et à Frédéric Barbey*, volume *II: 1914–1928*, eds. Françoise Dubosson et al., (Genève: Fondation Gustave Ador et Editions Slatkine, 2009), specifically letters number 334; 338; 347; 348; 350; 362; 370; 373; 377; 380; 383.
20 Melanie Oppenheimer, '"A golden moment?" [...]', 8–27.
21 *Procès verbaux entrevue des Croix-Rouges alliées et du Comité International à Genève*, 13 February 1919 in file 'Hors Inventaire' CR 30, ICRC archives, Geneva.
22 Unless otherwise indicated, the synthesis of information provided in this paragraph originates from *Procès verbaux entrevue des Croix-Rouges alliées et du Comité International à Genève*, 13 February 1919 in file 'Hors Inventaire' CR 30, ICRC archives, Geneva.
23 Oppenheimer and Collins, *Henry Pomeroy Davison 1867–1922*, 51.
24 ICRC minutes, 19 February 1919.
25 ICRC minutes, 26 February 1919.
26 ICRC minutes, 5 February 1919.
27 ICRC minutes, 8 February 1919.
28 Cédric Cotter, *(S')Aider pour survivre. Action humanitaire et neutralité suisse pendant la Première Guerre mondiale*, (Genève: Georg éditeur, 2017), 488–499.
29 ICRC minutes, 12 February 1919. Ador's apprehensiveness was not misplaced: Davison had expressed an ambition to reorganise the Red Cross and align the movement and its structure with the League of Nations. ICRC minutes, 26 February 1919.
30 ICRC minutes, 26 February 1919.
31 Romain Fathi, 'Sovereignty, Democracy and Neutrality [...]', 307–309.
32 ICRC minutes,12 February 1919.
33 Daniel Palmieri, 'Introduction', *Les Procès-Verbaux de l'Agence Internationale des Prisonniers de Guerre, volume 2* (Genève: CICR, 2014), 6.
34 ICRC minutes,12 February 1919.
35 See letters from General Pau (President of the Central Committee of the French Red Cross) to Alexandre Millerand (*Président du Conseil* and Minister for Foreign Affairs) on 12 February 1920; Millerand to Pau on 21 February 1920, and Pierre de Margerie (French Ambassador to Belgium) to Alexandre Millerand, 9 March 1920, in file *Unions Internationales* 1139, MAE, Courneuve.
36 Davison, *Proceedings*, 79.
37 Ibid.

38 'Discours de M. Edouard Naville, Président *ad interim* du Comité International à l'occasion de la réunion annuelle de la section genevoise de la Croix-Rouge', 2 avril 1919, *La Croix-Rouge Suisse. Revue mensuelle des Samaritains suisses, Soins des malades et hygiène populaire*, 1 September 1919.

39 Roger Durand, *'La Conférence Médicale de Cannes, ses participants et le Bulletin de la Ligue des Sociétés de la Croix-Rouge'*, 60.

40 Fathi and Oppenheimer, 'The Shôken Fund and the evolution of the Red Cross movement', 818–819.

Chapter 2

JUSTIFYING THE FIRST HUMANITARIAN INTERNATIONAL PUBLIC HEALTH ORGANISATION

This chapter provides some context to better understand the significance and outcomes of the Cannes Medical Conference. It does so by briefly reviewing medical conferences that preceded the Cannes Medical Conference and assessing where they had fallen short. Until Cannes, there had been no successful attempts to create a truly international non-government organisation to make recommendations and take action on the issue of global public health. This chapter historicises the thinking and the climate behind the creation of the first voluntary humanitarian and global public health organisation: the League of Red Cross Societies. The professional backgrounds of the delegates to the Cannes Medical Conference – some of the most eminent medical specialists of the time, including Nobel Prize winners – are presented in the second section of this chapter, as well as the chief organiser of the conference: Henry Pomeroy Davison and the role he played in designing it.

Medical Conferences Before Cannes: A Concise Background

Delegates to the Cannes Medical Conference understood its significance relative to prior conferences and organisations, which were recalled several times throughout the proceedings. For instance, American delegate and Professor of Hygiene and Public Health, William F. Snow, noted that 'the historic significance of this particular meeting [Cannes] should not be lost. It ranks with the conference in Brussels or the Conference in 1902 and 1904'.[1] This comparison with past scientific and medical conferences highlights how the Cannes Medical Conference inserted itself in the longer history of public health conferences. Indeed, the late nineteenth century saw conferences multiplying, including but not limited to major diplomatic, humanitarian and medical conferences that sought to resolve pressing issues of the time.² The conference format was accepted as a legitimate way to gather eminent specialists to address specific problems, and by the end of the First World War, it remained a valid and prestigious *modus operandi*.³ It is therefore unsurprising that the embryo from which the League of Red Cross Societies developed took the form of an international conference. What is noteworthy about the 1919 Cannes Medical Conference, however, is that, unlike most other medical conferences, it resulted in the creation of an organisation: the League of Red Cross Societies, which is still active today, albeit under a different name. Previous international medical conferences only resulted in more limited, yet notable outcomes that are worth briefly outlining here.

Before the Cannes Medical Conference of 1919, there were a number of international medical conferences, starting with the 1851 Paris International Sanitary Conference that focused on cholera. This initial gathering was followed by another eleven conferences until 1912, mostly held in Paris but also in Constantinople, Vienna, Washington, Rome, Dresden and Venice.⁴ Those conferences were attended by government officials, diplomats in particular, and aimed, for example, at harmonising regulations on quarantine and border crossing. They also considered specific diseases and problems of sanitation. Over the years, several projects were proposed to establish an International Sanitary Commission and an International Health Council, but to no avail.⁵ National politics often proved obstructive, and state representatives primarily sought to tackle health problems within national and imperial frameworks, rather than globally. In fact, it was only at the 1903 Paris conference that an article in a sanitary convention prompted the creation of the *Office International d'Hygiène Publique* (OIHP) in December 1907. But the principal aim of the OIHP was to collect and share medical information for and among signatory states only. As historians Marcos Cueto, Theodore Brown and Elizabeth Fee have noted, 'there was no intention to establish an organisation with executive powers or to intrude into the public health administration of the participating countries'.⁶ In fact, they further argue that the French-dominated institution sought primarily to protect select national populations from specific epidemics erupting in less developed countries, rather than to improve global public health.⁷

The International Health Commission of the Rockefeller Foundation, founded in 1913, was the first global initiative that sought to promote global public health. But the Commission, which took up a plethora of initiatives, remained a private project led by one organisation.⁸ The League of Red Cross Societies would become the first truly transnational, federated, non-governmental initiative that involved Red Cross national societies in its decision-making process and sought to serve global public health and, in doing so, abide by Red Cross principles. Its aims, programme of work and federated and democratic structure made it a non-governmental forerunner to the League of Nations Health Organisation created in 1920 and the World Health Organisation created in 1948.[9] While the League of Red Cross Societies' aims partly filtered through both aforementioned organisations, it is perhaps best understood through its uniqueness rather than the lineage to which it contributed, and this is because the League of Red Cross Societies had broader missions than public health, such as supporting the creation of new Red Cross Red Crescent national societies and the Junior Red Cross.

Delegates of the Cannes Medical Conference envisioned a future where the organisation that was to be born from the conference would work towards 'the betterment of the health and general welfare of the peoples of the world, without reference to race, nationality, color, or religious belief, particularly directing its activities at first to those peoples and in those areas where the need is most urgent'.[10] They acknowledged a number of times that the organisation would need to take into consideration local beliefs and customs, but they believed that science and medicine were universal. Although Red Crescent societies were not represented at Cannes, both the British and French empires colonised large swathes of the Muslim world and their national societies were involved in Muslim colonies and protectorates. Soon, Red Crescent national societies would join the League of Red Cross Societies: Iran and Egypt in 1929, Turkey in 1930 and Iraq in 1934. The real 'moment' for the League in the Muslim world started in earnest in the decolonisation era. From 1948 to the mid-1960s, many Red Crescent national societies became members of the League such as Pakistan, Syria, Jordan, Afghanistan, Tunisia, Libya and Algeria. From its inception at Cannes, the vision for the League was that of a universal organisation within which humanitarian assistance was not conceived to discriminate but to improve people's health across the globe.

Given that by the end of the First World War, there was no truly global, internationally recognised health organisation, it is unsurprising that at the opening of the 1919 Cannes Medical Conference, the delegates unanimously agreed that such an organisation was lacking and ought to be created as soon as possible in order to work towards the betterment of the world's health. This is why the delegates were invited to Cannes in the first place: to elaborate and develop a structure for such an organisation. They had a flurry of ideas and the sky soon became the limit as grandiose plans for the future organisation were voiced. To understand these plans and ideas and their substance, it is necessary to consider who the conference delegates and their host were.

Delegates to the Cannes Medical Conference and their Host, Henry Pomeroy Davison

Sixty official delegates (listed in Appendix) attended the Cannes Medical Conference from 1 to 11 April 1919, of whom only eight were women, all associated with nursing.[11] Delegates were invited by Davison's Committee of Red Cross Societies, and their stay in Cannes was fully funded through a $2.5 million appropriation, which Davison had received from the American Red Cross to establish the League of Red Cross Societies.[12] With the exception of two American delegates, a former ambassador and a representative of the American Red Cross, all other fifty-eight delegates had a medical background: they were doctors, professors, head nurses or medical practitioners in world-leading institutes and organisations. Of the sixty delegates, sixteen were associated with their national armies, most of whom had medical expertise. A few were also high-level representatives of Red Cross national societies but again, those delegates generally had a medical background. The French Red Cross was the least represented, with only one French Red Cross representative in the twelve-member French delegation. This was because Davison preferred to invite French medical experts who had previously worked with American colleagues and were supportive of American projects,[13] and also because the French Red Cross did not want to change the status quo whereby only the ICRC, so far, had had the power and legitimacy to call for international Red Cross conferences.[14] It was therefore reluctant to send more representatives to Cannes.

Cannes itself was chosen for multiple reasons. The Paris Peace Conference was so large that finding accommodation and transport in and around Paris in the first half of 1919 was notoriously difficult. The British delegation alone was spread across five large hotels near the Arc de Triomphe, and there were dozens of delegations with diplomats, ministers and heads of state that needed lodging suited to their status.[15] Besides accommodation, the conference format required small rooms for section work and a large room for plenary sessions. Finding an appropriate venue in Paris or its region would have been even more complicated, also due to the ongoing Peace Conference. Cannes, which Davison knew already, had lovely weather at that time of the year and was a known holidaying location for royalty, aristocracy and the elites ever since the late nineteenth century.[16] In 1919, receiving an invitation to attend a conference at Cannes' *Cercle Nautique* – originally a very exclusive yacht club and one of the city's most luxurious and well-known premises – would have been a very attractive proposition for invited delegates, one synonymous with prestige, the health benefits of a warmer climate, and first-class entertainment and dining options. Cannes' distance to Paris also meant that political interference would be limited, which was perhaps the greatest benefit of all. Furthermore, Cannes would act as a retreat where delegates would stay with one another for just under a fortnight, a set-up conducive to greater productivity and socialisation.

The profiles of the delegates at Cannes meant that the conference was a gathering of medical experts (Figure 1), rather than diplomats or state representatives. This was Davison's vision for the conference precisely because he knew that political intervention was unlikely to deliver the outcome he desired. Besides, the latter groups of professionals did not have the scientific knowledge required to establish a legitimate programme for the future League. The largest delegation at Cannes came from the United States of America, with nineteen delegates, followed by Britain and France with twelve each, Italy with ten, and Japan with two. Amongst the delegates, listed in Appendix, were three Nobel Laureates in medicine (Ronald Ross, Camillo Golgi and Alphonse Laveran), members of prestigious academies and institutes and leading medical figures of the time, some of whom had pre-existing connections with one another.[17] With such qualifications and international recognition, this learned assembly was eminently appropriate to address and make recommendations on medical issues put to them: they were at the forefront of their profession and their expertise could not

Figure 1 Some of the Cannes Medical Conference's delegates, with Henry Pomeroy Davison seated at the front, third from the left. Note the number of people in uniform.

be questioned.[18] Some were known public figures, with long-standing connections with their state, army and Red Cross national societies. They represented the type of legitimacy Davison was after to justify the League's creation. If he and his closest associates shepherded them to produce reports on actions, treatments and prevention measures to take against specific health problems, no government, organisation or Red Cross society would have the expertise or legitimacy to go against such recommendations established by a transnational group of experts.

In his opening address on the first day of the conference, Davison explained that he wished to bring together scientists 'recognized as leaders of the world in [their] specialities' to create a new programme for the Red Cross in times of peace, the organisation having proven its global usefulness in times of war. Speaking to his assembly, Davison asked: 'now what is there to do? [...] shall we demobilise'?[19] Davison explained that he had presented his vision for a Committee of Red Cross Societies – the future League of Red Cross Societies – to President Wilson who 'at once grasped the force and importance of the suggestion and asked that I devote myself to doing what I could to see that the plan was formulated and carried out'.[20] Davison further impressed upon his audience that his ideas and presidential mandate to create such a new organisation were well received by leaders of the British, Canadian, French, Italian and Japanese Red Cross societies who were discussing the post-war period and how their organisations might remain useful to society. Davison explained that he had arranged for Wilson to ask that governmental support of the idea be secured from the Allies, and Wilson had obliged. The French, British and Italian Prime ministers '[notified their] respective Red Cross organization[s] that [they] regarded this movement [the future League] as one of very great importance'.[21] But Davison wanted to stress that his proposed movement was not an American movement, nor that the number of supporters assembled was definitive. Quite the contrary. He envisaged his Committee of Red Cross Societies as a 'nucleus', an 'initial start' that would expand to include other national societies, thus creating a need for an organisation that would co-ordinate the public health work of the Red Cross Red Crescent movement at an international level, what would become the League of Red Cross Societies. Davison further elaborated that his ambition was to multiply the number of Red Cross national societies across the globe so that the League would eventually become a true 'forum for the world', sharing scientific knowledge across borders, peoples and religions.[22]

A noteworthy orator, Davison pointed out that it was now or never, that now was the 'psychological moment' because people across the world knew that the Red Cross had been a force for good during the war, that the Paris Peace Conference was redesigning the world's order, that reconstruction needed to be undertaken, and that epidemics like the Spanish Flu were fresh in peoples' memories or ongoing.[23] Davison explained: 'We know the public wants this, and I know, as Dr. Roux [an eminent French delegate and the conference's President] also told me himself, that if we did not do this someone else would. The world demands it, and what we are going to do is just to crystallize that demand'.[24] If the Red Cross were to demobilise instead of finding a new programme of work, all its resources, capacities, volunteers and personnel would evaporate, which was inconceivable for Davison, as it was to members of Red Cross national societies around the world.

The conference's programme was designed with a specific goal: the establishment of written measures that would provide scientifically approved actionable items to the yet-to-be-established League of Red Cross Societies. The conference had general sessions but was organised and subdivided into working parties called 'sections'. During the general sessions, all delegates assembled to hear the various reports produced by each section and to discuss broad topics such as the establishment of a central (that is, international) bureau of health, the shape it might take, and its possible prerogatives and means of action. Such general sessions provided an opportunity for consensus to emerge and be duly noted by Davison. Section work, however, was perhaps the most important work carried out at Cannes. Each section involved specific specialists on the topic at hand, and their mission was to formulate practical guidelines, resolutions or recommendations to address specific health issues. Such sections included: venereal diseases, child welfare, tuberculosis, malaria, nursing, preventive medicine and the last section was called publication, education and statistics. Some of those issues were scourges of the time, but they were also spaces in which some Red Cross national societies worked during, and at times even before, the First World War. This book will later turn to the work produced by the conference's sections (Chapter 5) and how it was mobilised to create the League of Red Cross Societies and provide it with work to do. For now, however, Davison's central role in shaping the future League of Red Cross Societies, and his connections to American President Woodrow Wilson, raises an important question. Was the Cannes Medical Conference – and therefore the future League of Red Cross Societies – an American-led initiative or a 'natural development' for the Red Cross movement? The following chapter aims to answer that question.

Notes

1 Snow, *Proceedings*, 84.
2 Claude Tapia and Jacques Taieb, 'Conférences et Congrès Internationaux de 1815 à 1913', *Relations Internationales* 4, no. 5 (1976): 11–35.

3 See, for example, the 1989 special issue of *Mil neuf cent* titled 'Les congrès lieux de l'échange intellectuel 1850–1914' and Anne Rasmussen, 'Jalons Pour Une Histoire Des Congrès Internationaux au XIXe Siècle : Régulation Scientifique et Propagande Intellectuelle', *Relations Internationales* 62 (1990): 115–133.
4 Norman Howard-Jones, *Les bases scientifiques des Conférences sanitaires internationales 1851–1938* (Genève: Organisation Mondiale de la Santé, 1975). On these conferences, see also: Valeska Huber, 'The Unification of the Globe by Disease? The International Sanitary Conferences on Cholera, 1851–1894', *The Historical Journal* 49, no. 2 (2006): 453–476.
5 Marcos Cueto, Theodore M. Brown and Elizabeth Fee, *The World Health Organization: A History* (Cambridge: Cambridge University Press, 2019), 15.
6 Ibid.
7 Ibid., 16. See also Howard-Jones, *Les bases scientifiques* [...], 94–97.
8 John Farley, *To Cast Out Disease: A History of the International Health Division of Rockefeller Foundation (1913–1951)* (New York: Oxford University Press, 2004), 2–4 and 27–43.
9 There are of course vast differences between the League of Red Cross Societies and those two organisations, but the League was part of that ecosystem of proto-international health organisations that contributed to demonstrating the necessity of international governmental health organisations. Establishing the degree of lineage between the *Office Internationale d'Hygiène Publique*, the International Health Committee of the Rockefeller Foundation, the League of Red Cross Societies, the League of Nations Health Organisation and the World Health Organisation is perhaps not as important as acknowledging that these bodies were not created in a vacuum and that they each played a role in pushing peoples and states alike toward considering international public health as a major function for government.
10 *Proceedings*, 43. An idea reiterated on page 71.
11 For Britain, Miss Gill, superintendent at Edinburgh's Nurses' Royal Infirmary and Miss Lloyd-Still, Head Matron at London's St. Thomas Hospital; for France, Countess de Roussy de Sales, Head Nurse for the *Société de Secours aux Blessés Militaires*; for Italy, Professor Malatesta Anselmi, Rome's inspector of voluntary nurses, Countess Gigliucci, nurse of the Italian Red Cross and for the United States, Miss Hall, Chief Nurse American Red Cross in France; Miss Stimson, Director of the American Expeditionary Force's Army Nurse Corps and Miss Wald, Representative of the Federal Children's Bureau of the US Department of Labor.
12 'League of Red Cross Societies Miscellaneous records, Financial Statements', Box 1, Folder 15, Hoover Institution Library & Archives. See also Oppenheimer and Collins, *Henry Pomeroy Davison*, 89.
13 Those connections are traced in Jean Guillermand, 'La Croix-Rouge américaine et le corps médical français', 101–109. Representatives of the French Red Cross had been directed by their government to support Davison's project although they were ambivalent about it. Romain Fathi, 'Sovereignty, Democracy and Neutrality [...]', 308–309. By 1919, Davison's relationship with the French was not at its strongest. See: Michael E. McGuire, 'At (Red) Cross Purposes: American Red Cross Humanitarian "Arrogance" and France's Great War Relief and Reconstruction, 1917–20.' *European Review of History: Revue Européenne d'histoire* 30, no. 5 (2023): 705–726.
14 French Red Cross Vice President Amiral Touchard to ICRC President *ad interim* Edouard Naville, 6 February 1919, in file 'Conférence de Genève Février 1919', CR 30–1, ICRC archives, Geneva. The French Red Cross was fearful of increased

American influence over the Red Cross movement. On this influence in a broader context, please see Bridget Towers, 'Red Cross Organisational Politics, 1918–1922: Relations of Dominance and the Influence of the United States' in *International Health Organisations and Movements, 1918–1939*, ed. Paul Weindling, (Cambridge: Cambridge University Press, 1995), 36–55.
15 Margaret Macmillan, *Paris 1919. Six Months the Changed the World* (London: John Murray, 2019), 53.
16 Nicole Renoir, 'Le Cercle Nautique à Cannes 1864–1947' in *La Conférence Médicale de Cannes*, ed. Roger Durand, (Genève: Société Henry Dunant, 1994), 23–35.
17 A full list of the conference delegates is available in the *Proceedings*, with the names, titles and professions of the delegates.
18 It has been noted that while by all accounts, even for their peers, the delegates at Cannes represented the elite of medical professions, the gathering excluded representatives from other allied countries, neutral countries and, evidently, enemy countries thus depriving the conference from notable experts in other countries. Guillermand, 'La Croix-Rouge américaine et le corps médical français', 110–112.
19 Davison, *Proceedings*, 18.
20 Ibid.
21 Ibid., 19
22 Ibid., 21–22.
23 Davison, *Proceedings*, 21. Delegates did not dwell on the recent Influenza pandemic: it was neither ignored nor central to their discussions. It is mentioned less than a handful of times through the *Proceedings* but Davison does make the case that had the institution he envisioned existed then, it could perhaps have prevented the disease or 'at least lessen [its] seriousness of character'.
24 Ibid., 48.

Chapter 3

AN AMERICAN INITIATIVE OR A 'NATURAL EVOLUTION' FOR THE RED CROSS MOVEMENT?

The Cannes Medical Conference can be located within what some have called the 'Wilsonian moment': a time that saw a reconfiguration of the world order. As the First World War drew to an end, centuries-old empires collapsed while the United States emerged as a leading global power and sought to redefine international relations.[1] US President Woodrow Wilson championed the creation of the League of Nations, and the League of Red Cross Societies was set to become its non-governmental humanitarian counterpart. Although there had otherwise been a transnational evolution among some of the Red Cross national societies that were already active in peacetime work before the First World War, driving the whole movement towards public health was spearheaded by the American Red Cross in the aftermath of the conflict. The chapter argues that the League of Red Cross Societies was not a revolution for the Red Cross movement, but an evolution, an expansion in a context of global post-war health emergency and identity crisis for Red Cross national societies. That evolution was catalysed by vision, energy and money made in the United States of America, an American leadership that resulted in the creation of the League of Red Cross Societies somewhat paradoxically enabled by the ICRC's reluctance to transform itself. The Cannes Medical Conference took place within a swift interim, after the guns had fallen silent but before the signing of the peace treaties; a time when humanity could dream of different futures and think about its next war: that against disease, one which would be led outside the governmental space, specifically by the League of Red Cross Societies.

A Wilsonian Moment for the Red Cross

Although the terminology 'Wilsonian moment' has been debated, its heuristic value is helpful to reflect on the influence of the United States on the reshaping of the post-war world.[2] In essence, Wilsonianism was a vision for liberal internationalism that challenged the continuation of the pre-First World War imperial world order and its tenets. Wilsonianism 'expressed the values of democracy and capitalism, including freedom and human rights'.[3] Although some critics have pointed to the degree of idealism that underpinned Wilsonianism, and to the fact that it was not universal at that point in time, key principles included 'national self-determination, [...] democratic self-government; [...] [and] Open door economic globalization'.[4] The vision, foundation and organisational structure of the League of Red Cross Societies very much form part of this moment, when people like Wilson and Davison genuinely thought that a new world order could be established based on these values.[5] Davison rode on this presidential mandate, on the aura of the United States of America whose industrial and financial might had taken the world by surprise.[6] At the Cannes Medical Conference, that connection to the Wilsonian project was also made clear by another delegate, Dr. William H. Welch, Director of the School of Hygiene and Public Health at Johns Hopkins University and President of the Board of Scientific Directors of the Rockefeller Institute for Medical Research, former President of the National Academy of Science and ex-advisor to the US Army's medical department. Welch provided the American delegation's opening address expressing his, and 'that of the entire medical profession of America['s]', total support for Davison's great plan. He added: 'there are assembled in Paris delegates to consider the formation of a League of Nations. We are assembled here to confer upon the formation of a League of Health'.[7] Welch envisioned that such a League of Health 'under the Associated Red Cross Societies of the World' would support the work of the League of Nations and perhaps be placed under its direction. Certainly, 'the League of Red Cross Societies format also reinforced Wilson's belief in the League [of Nations] as the arbiter of an American-as-global international order'.[8] There is no doubt that the League of Red Cross Societies was a humanitarian project, but its political underpinnings and associations cannot be ignored.[9] It fitted in and contributed to a period of 'Americanization' of humanitarian aid.[10] As with previous medical conferences discussed in Chapter 2, the push for its establishment came from large, powerful, imperialist economic powerhouses. These were far from constituting a monolithic bloc: there was much competition between the British and French empires, both of which had been considerably shaken by the First World War, and the leadership of the United States, Japan and Italy was on the rise, keen to challenge the world order that had been established mostly without them across previous centuries.

While Davison had a broader project for the League of Red Cross Societies than public health exclusively, he campaigned actively to secure a League of Nations mandate for the future League of Red Cross Societies. This mandate was inscribed in Article 25 of the Covenant of the League of Nations that stated: 'The Members of the League agree to encourage and promote the establishment and co-operation of duly authorised voluntary Red Cross national organisations having as purposes the improvement of health, the prevention of disease and the mitigation of suffering throughout the world'.[11] This was a smart move for both Wilson and Davison. For Wilson, it meant civil society support for his League of Nations project, while for Davison, it granted the League of Red Cross Societies an official mandate to become a new international Red Cross institution if the ICRC was not willing to take on Article 25.[12] The Cannes Medical Conference tells us that the League of Red Cross Societies, as both a project and an institution, was very much a concrete outcome of what has been named the 'Wilsonian moment', and one that long survived Wilson's ambitions and Wilson himself.[13]

An American Initiative or a 'Natural Development' for the Red Cross World?

American paternity of the League of Red Cross Societies may be clear, but as with the League of Nations, the elements that underpinned it were not an American invention. In other words, the birth of the League of Nations and that of the League of Red Cross Societies may well be credited to or associated with the Wilsonian moment, but they are more accurately described as points of arrival rather than points of departure, accomplishments rather than revolutions. Ideals that predicated the League of Nations were by 1919 at least a couple of centuries old,[14] and the public health turn of the Red Cross movement had started to occur at the national level well before the First World War.[15] Its globalisation under unified leadership was the innovation, not so much the nature of the work to perform. Davison was well aware of this. Although he generally remained quiet during the conference (at least in its published proceedings), he urged his audience to create a transnational peacetime Red Cross organisation that would work toward the betterment of public health, which he saw as a natural development for the Red Cross. He declared that 'an Italian Professor had proposed in a pamphlet [...] published in 1909, an International Association of Red Cross Organisations for the benefit of mankind, with particular reference to the prevention of disease', stressing that 'it proved the fact that there is nothing new under the sun, and that the present movement really began in Italy'.[16] Davison was also well aware that the Japanese, American, French, British and other Red Cross national societies had ventured into and supported public health initiatives before the war, mentioning such initiatives several times throughout the proceedings.[17] Emphasising the Italian example, he wanted to point out that his idea of a peacetime international Red Cross movement taking up the cause of public health was not a uniquely American idea, nor a first. This was important because some in the audience conceived Davison's grand project as an American initiative. In as much as the personalities of the delegates can come through the formal character of edited proceedings of a professional conference, American delegates very much felt that they had to convince the attendees that the project was not all American. One of them, Livingston Farrand, the Chairman of the Central Committee of the American Red Cross, as he was about to speak first apologised saying 'I am extremely reluctant to add another American voice to this discussion', a rather revealing preamble.[18] At Cannes, the American delegation was the largest, the conference was paid for by money obtained by Davison from the American Red Cross, and the future League of Red Cross Societies was being placed into the fold of the League of Nations, itself not a new idea but this time around promoted by the United States. The whole context was very Americanised at a time when the world's largest two empires, Britain and France, and also Italy, were acutely aware of the financial and military debts they owed to the United States of America.

Emphasising the American paternity of the League of Red Cross Societies should not, however, diminish the fact that Davison was correct in this instance: the idea of an international Red Cross existing in times of peace and developing a programme of public health work was not new, and the Italians were not the only ones who had proposed it before the war. The Japanese Red Cross had long advocated for such a programme to be endorsed by the ICRC and other national societies. It did so at the VII, VIII and IX International Conferences of the Red Cross, respectively, in St. Petersburg in 1902, London in 1907 and Washington in 1912.[19] What was new in 1919, however, was the emergence of the United States of America as a global superpower with unprecedented means to influence international affairs, although it was a path America would not follow after Warren G. Harding took up residence in the White House in 1921. But during the Cannes Medical Conference, which was happening alongside the most important event of the time – the Paris Peace Conference – all eyes were on Wilson, his 14 points (a series of key principles that would help draft a lasting peace), the League of Nations, and American initiatives, including those in the non-governmental space.

Predictably, some delegates perceived the Cannes Medical Conference as primarily an American rather than a transnational initiative. Regardless of the degree of legitimacy of such a feeling, what is clear is that it is precisely because Davison's idea had previously been tested or implemented at a national level by the five Red Cross national societies which formed the nucleus of the League of Red Cross Societies (besides others as well that would later join it), that the constitution of this League could be supported in 1919. In fact, other delegates also envisaged this new programme of work as an extension of the work of the Red Cross, rather than a revolutionary project. American delegate Dr. Welch presented the League of Red Cross Societies project as a 'natural and logical path of development'[20] for the Red Cross movement, a 'natural evolution of the work of relief adapted to peace conditions for the welfare of mankind'.[21] Delegates from other countries expressed the same feeling throughout the proceedings. That idea was so prevalent during the Cannes Medical Conference that the creation of the League of Red Cross Societies was described several times, conveniently perhaps, as an inevitable development. It must be noted, however, that this feeling of inevitability expanded well beyond the Cannes Conference delegates. The idea was widely circulated in the European and Northern American press at the time under the name, or its variations, of *Croix-Rouge de la Paix*, the Red Cross of Peace, or Peacetime Red Cross. The ICRC, which was monitoring such developments closely, kept an entire file in its archives with press clippings from a wide range of newspapers.[22] The genie was out of the bottle, and many were advocating for its materialisation.

This materialisation, however, was undoubtedly made in the United States of America. The transnational evolution that had taken place within the Red Cross movement crystallised thanks to American leadership and funding. To be sure, much of the League of Red Cross Societies' early structure and areas of work were conceptualised and mapped out by Davison before Cannes, with the help of his ally, Dr. Richard P. Strong, Director of the Medical Research Department of the American Red Cross, Professor at Harvard's Medical School and, crucially, US representative to the Interallied Sanitary Commission in Paris.[23] Strong had a broad view of global sanitary issues of the time and drafted, ahead of the conference, the central memorandum circulated to conference delegates and that prefigured the League. Cannes was as much a consultation of medical experts as it was a formality to demonstrate that an institution such as the League of Red Cross Societies was needed. The summary of the conference's proceedings notes that 'the conclusion was reached that it was a natural and most desirable evolution for the Red Cross to extend its functions of relief during war to that of promoting public health during peace'.[24]

The general introductory statement to the conference delegates' overall recommendations and resolutions, also presented at the beginning of the proceedings, fully adopted Davison's language, and fully endorsed and 'approve[d] of the purpose of the Committee of Red Cross Societies to extend greatly the activity of the Red Cross in time of peace, for the prevention of disease and the betterment of the health and general welfare of the people in all countries'.[25] This came after laudatory words on the relief work of the Red Cross during the war as a proven 'agency for good of unparalleled force and power'.[26] The expansion of wartime Red Cross work to public health in peacetime was again presented as a 'logical development' for the Red Cross movement.[27] The proceedings, published in 1919, served to justify the founding of the League of Red Cross Societies, recording that everyone present agreed with Davison's plan to expand the work of the Red Cross movement to peacetime and public health work. For Dr. Wickliffe Rose, another American and the then Director of the International Health Board of the Rockefeller Foundation, the birth of this new international Red Cross organisation was both a 'fundamental necessity' and 'inevitable': 'Horrible as this war has been, I am inclined to think we are going, some day, to come to look upon it as the birth pangs of a new world order established upon much brighter lines'.[28] Wickliffe Rose insisted that work in the field of disease prevention was nothing new for the Red Cross, but an extension of previous work which instead of being carried out at a national level would be executed at the global level through transnational cooperation.

Besides the American delegation, the Italian delegation was the most enthusiastic and supportive of Davison's vision.[29] Its representative Dr. Marchiafava, the Vice President of the Italian Red Cross, explained that the public health work of the proposed new institution was something that the Italian Red Cross had done for over twenty years in Italy. To members of the Italian delegation as well, the proposed organisation seemed like a natural extension of Red Cross work.[30] In fact, when tuberculosis was discussed, an Italian delegate explained that the Italian Red Cross 'has made this its programme of peace, the very reason for its future existence, and can only applaud the initiative of the American Red Cross which tries to-day to unite all the Red Cross Societies of the world'.[31] But one also wonders if such manifest support towards Davison and, therefore, towards the American Red Cross, was also the outcome of the latter's significant support to the Italian Red Cross during the war when the American Red Cross became a major humanitarian player on the Italian front and throughout Italy.[32] Italian delegate Dr. Castellani made a passionate plea to expand the work of the Red Cross into peacetime, asking the participants if any of them knew of diseases that stopped during war or peace, making the point that they were rampant irrespective of either, and concluded that diseases were a 'continuous calamity'.[33] Overall, the British, Japanese and French delegations were also supportive of Davison's project, although the latter twice made it clear that French doctors would not collaborate with former enemy nations.[34] In this, French delegates adopted their government's position in excluding former enemies, Germany in particular, from the reconstruction of the world order. Science and medicine were not sheltered from nationalism and indeed during the conflict, scientists had heavily fed the war propaganda machines of their respective countries.[35]

There's no doubt that the Italian and Japanese Red Cross societies played an important role at the Cannes Medical Conference and in supporting the creation of the League of Red Cross Societies. Like the American Red Cross, these national societies were forerunners when it came to the diversification of Red Cross activities to support civilians. Both societies had advocated for a peacetime Red Cross before the First World War and their representatives at Cannes agreed with Davison that now was the time to turn the movement towards public health, relief and other non-war-related activities that would alleviate and could at times prevent the suffering of populations.

All in all, when thinking about what prompted the League's establishment, several key factors can be identified. The first of them, the one that made its coming into being possible, is that in terms of Red Cross work, the League did not represent a revolution but an evolution, an expansion. As explained, several national societies had delved into forms of public health work well before the First World War. It is that experience that made many in the Red Cross movement supportive of the idea of a *Croix-Rouge de la Paix*, which the League was to embody. The second factor is context. The world faced a post-war health emergency at the same time that Red Cross national societies were facing a potential identity crisis. Created to alleviate suffering during war, what were they to become after the war to end all wars? To remain relevant, they needed to broaden the scope of their activities, and the global public health emergency, with the Spanish flu and other scourges, provided an avenue to pivot wartime medical aid to peacetime public health work. The third factor that contributed to the establishment of the League was, undeniably, American leadership in the Wilsonian moment. Without Wilson, without Davison and without the support of the American Red Cross, there is no doubt that the League of Red Cross Societies would not have been created in 1919 – perhaps even not at all – and certainly not with the federation-style governance structure that it adopted. Finally, the fourth major factor that explains the League's creation is the reluctance of the ICRC to take on that role within the movement and integrate these new public health, relief, and Junior Red Cross missions into its own work.

Notes

1 Adam Tooze, *The Deluge. The Great War and the Remaking of Global Order* (London: Allen Lane, 2014), 199–231.
2 On this notion, see Erez Manela, *The Wilsonian Moment Self-Determination and the International Origins of Anticolonial Nationalism* (Oxford: Oxford University Press, 2007). The creation of the League of Red Cross Societies can be contextualised in this short-lived yet ambitious 'Wilsonian moment' that was characteristically tinged with a degree of idealism itself somewhat produced by the context of the end of a world war.

Clyde F. Buckingham has documented Wilson's involvement with and vision for the creation of the League, see also John F. Hutchinson, *Champions of Charity*, 285–290.

3 Lloyd E. Ambrosius, *Wilsonianism: Woodrow Wilson and His Legacy in American Foreign Relations* (New York: Palgrave Macmillan, 2002), 1.

4 Ibid., 2; 1–48. See also: Trygve Throntveit, *Power without Victory. Woodrow Wilson and the American Internationalist Experiment* (Chicago: The University of Chicago Press, 2017) and Jeremy Menchik, 'Woodrow Wilson and the Spirit of Liberal Internationalism', *Politics, Religion & Ideology* 22, no. 2 (2021): 231–253.

5 On ideologies at play in the Red Cross Red Crescent movement, see: Jean-François Fayet, 'Humanitaire et Communisme: histoires parallèles et croisées' in Jean-François Fayet, Marie-Luce Desgrandchamps, Marie Cugnet et Donia Hasler, *La Croix face à l'Etoile Rouge: Humanitaire et Communisme au XXe siècle*, (Geneva: Georg: forthcoming).

6 Davison to Axson, 21 March 1919, 'League of Red Cross Societies Miscellaneous records', Box 1, Folder 8, Hoover Institution Library & Archives. During the conference Davison made sure to keep Wilson informed about his 'plans', 'in interest of [Wilson's] world project', arranging for Stockton Axson to act as direct liaison with the President. Axson was Wilson's brother-in-law from Wilson's first marriage and the National Secretary of the American Red Cross.

7 Welch, *Proceedings*, 25.

8 We thank one of the anonymous reviewers for this observation made during the peer reviewing process.

9 They were certainly clear to the Soviets. See Jean-François Fayet, 'D'une ambivalente hostilité à une distante adhésion: La Croix-Rouge soviétique et la Ligue des Sociétés de la Croix-Rouge durant l'entre-deux-guerre'.

10 Julia F. Irwin, 'The Disaster of War: American Understandings of Catastrophe, Conflict and Relief', *First World War Studies* 5, no. 1, (2014): 18, and Kimberly A. Lowe, 'The League of Red Cross Societies and International Committee of the Red Cross: a Re-Evaluation of American Influence in Interwar Internationalism', *Moving the Social* 57 (2017): 38.

11 The Covenant is available at: https://avalon.law.yale.edu/20th_century/leagcov.asp#art25 [accessed 10 January 2023]. Davison is the one who pushed for this article within the Covenant. Cutler to Davison, 2 April 1919, 'League of Red Cross Societies Miscellaneous records', Box 1, Folder 8, Hoover Institution Library & Archives.

12 Melanie Oppenheimer has explained that the British delegation at the Paris Peace Conference made sure that the League of Nations could develop its own health programs beyond its association with the League of Red Cross Societies. Melanie Oppenheimer, '"A golden moment?"...', 21.

13 It must be noted that the *Proceedings* make no mention of Bolshevism, communism or the Russian revolution, perhaps because the perceived threat to the established order was all too present in the minds of the League's initiators. Only an 'informal session of the conference' called for action in Central Europe and the East to tackle Typhus fever. *Proceedings*, 162–164. Bruno Cabanes has noted that America's fear of the expansion of communism was one of the factors that contributed to the ARC's redeployment from Western to Eastern Europe in late 1918 early 1919. Bruno Cabanes, *The Great War and the Origins of Humanitarianism, 1914–1924* (Cambridge: Cambridge University Press, 2014), 195, 213, 240. See also Jean-François Fayet, 'D'une ambivalente hostilité à une distante adhésion: La Croix-Rouge soviétique et la Ligue des Sociétés de la Croix-Rouge durant l'entre-deux-guerre' in Jean-François

Fayet, Marie-Luce Desgrandchamps, Marie Cugnet et Donia Hasler, *La Croix face à l'Etoile Rouge: Humanitaire et Communisme au XXe siècle*, (Geneva: Georg: forthcoming).
14 Jean-Michel Guieu, *Le rameau et le glaive. Les militants français pour la Société des Nations* (Paris: Les Presses de Sciences Po, 2008), 18–26.
15 Even the ICRC kept a file on national societies' peacetime and public health activities prior to the First World War. See 'Activité des Croix-Rouges en temps de paix. Historique', CR 103, ICRC archives, Geneva.
16 Davison, *Proceedings*, 109.
17 Curiously perhaps Davison does not discuss the pre-war peacetime and public health work of the Swiss Red Cross which was already well-developed, in the fight against tuberculosis in particular. As early as 1907, the monthly publication of the Swiss Red Cross drops the word 'militaire' from its title to insert 'soins des malades et hygiène populaire'. Davison probably did not know about this, as his relationship with the Swiss Red Cross was not as close or well informed as that which he had developed with the American, Italian, British and French Red Cross national societies during the war.
18 Livingston Farrand, *Proceedings*, 66.
19 Romain Fathi and Melanie Oppenheimer, 'The Shôken Fund and the evolution of the Red Cross movement', 815–817.
20 Welch, *Proceedings*, 50.
21 Ibid., 41.
22 File 'Croix-Rouge de la Paix. Coupures', CR 29-1, ICRC archives, Geneva.
23 Dr. Richard P. Strong, Director of the Medical Research Department of the American Red Cross, Professor at Harvard's Medical School and US representative to the Interallied Sanitary Commission in Paris had a key role in the planning of the Cannes Medical Conference and the shaping of the discussions that occurred there. Some of this work is preserved in the 'planning 1919' sub-file available in Z000363, IFRC archives, Geneva.
24 Preface, *Proceedings*, 2.
25 Recommendations and Resolutions of the Conference, *Proceedings*, 12.
26 Ibid.
27 Ibid.
28 Wickliffe Rose, *Proceedings*, 59.
29 Davison received a triumphant welcome in Rome where he addressed the population in the Coliseum on 7 April 1918. See Oppenheimer and Collins, *Henry Pomeroy Davison*, 42.
30 Marchiafava, *Proceedings*, 26.
31 'Report of Work of the Italian Red Cross in the Fight Against Tuberculosis Submitted to the Section on Tuberculosis', *Proceedings*, 128.
32 Daniela Rossini, 'The Activity and Influence of the American Red Cross in Italy during and after World War One (1917–1919)', *European Review of History: Revue Européenne d'histoire* 30, no. 5 (2023): 685–704.
33 Castellani, *Proceedings*, 40.
34 Roux, *Proceedings*, 167.
35 See for example Juliette Courmont, *L'odeur de l'ennemi. L'imaginaire olfactif en 1914–1918* (Paris: Armand Colin, 2010), 100–134; Roy Macleod, 'Scientists' in *The Cambridge History of the First World War*, ed. Jay Winter, (Cambridge: Cambridge University Press, 2014), 434–459.

Chapter 4

KNOWLEDGE IS THE CURE

This chapter focusses on the enthusiasm of the conference delegates for the founding of a global health organisation: the future League of Red Cross Societies. It investigates the differences in visions that conference delegates and Davison had over the shape and functions of the organisation that they were hoping would be born from Cannes. Although Davison's plan would prevail, investigating these differences is fruitful to think about how the Cannes Medical Conference served to legitimise a future organisation whose architecture had been conceived on the other side of the Atlantic before the delegates assembled. A central point of agreement in the debates held to define a future global organisation that would have public health as part of its mission statement was the importance of the circulation and dissemination of medical knowledge. This chapter reveals why the Cannes Medical Conference placed so much emphasis on the sharing of knowledge between experts at international level, as well as the sharing of basic medical and public health knowledge with local populations, through branches of Red Cross national societies. It shows how the circulation of scientific knowledge was a major driving force for the creation of the League of Red Cross Societies and its missions, representing the dawn of a new era for the Red Cross movement and global public health.

Channelling Conference Delegates' Enthusiasm

Besides their medical background, there are two observations one can make about the delegates of the Cannes Medical Conference. The first is that delegates were all supportive – if not extremely enthusiastic – of the need to create a new institution as envisaged by Davison. Asking medical staff if there was a need for a transnational organisation to improve global public health would hardly have resulted in a different opinion. From a corporatist point of view, and after five years of domination of the military and war effort (which also benefited the medical class), it is understandable that the profession would seek to advance its relevance to peoples' everyday lives in the aftermath of the conflict. The second observation is that from an analysis of the proceedings, there was virtually no disagreement among the delegates. During section work, delegates generally corroborated one another's recommendations. This type of general agreement could not have been achieved with politicians, diplomats or even national Red Cross representatives.[1] That is not to say that science or medicine was a universal language with no disagreement, but in this instance, delegates were always mindful of national contexts and acknowledged the research carried out by foreign colleagues. At Cannes, Science was most definitely a 'unifier', as Davison had hoped.[2] States' representatives were absent from the gathering because they were not invited, specifically because Davison was convinced that he would get broader agreement on how to tackle key health issues of the time through men and women of science, in turn giving a clear mandate for the new institution he had in mind, one that would rise above and beyond the politics of the immediate post-war period.

What Davison perhaps did not anticipate was the delegates' enthusiasm for a global health organisation whose aims would go far beyond what he was advocating. After his initial address, two projects were put forward to delegates in plenary sessions. They were called memoranda and presented for discussion. Both were presented by American delegates, Dr. Strong for the most elaborate one, and Dr. Biggs for the shorter memorandum, both heavily reflecting Davison's vision for the new organisation. Davison, although he was pulling the strings of the conference, remained mostly quiet in the proceedings after his opening speech because his ideas were predominantly voiced by American delegates Drs. Strong, Welch and Biggs, who had medical expertise.[3] This was arranged ahead of the conference, and Strong played a key role in drafting the conference programme, memoranda and outlines to be considered by delegates whom he also contributed to select.[4] The main memoranda were openly discussed by the delegates in the first sessions of the conference, and rather early on Davison had to refocus the work of the group, restate the conference's priorities, and appease the zeal of the delegates who were genuinely enthusiastic about being given a platform to conceptualise and structure the future of international health. Davison's project was Red Cross-focused and expanded beyond public health. He explained: 'If there were to-day in every country an effective, intelligent Red Cross organisation with the knowledge that each of us has, there would be no need for a Central Health Bureau [one of the many names used by delegates to conceptualise the future organisation]'.[5] For Davison, 'the importance lies within the country and not in the *Central Bureau* [Davison's emphasis]'.[6] For him, the point was not to create a central organisation that would work top to bottom, and certainly, it should not be a prototype for the centralised regulation-heavy organisation some delegates were advocating for. Davison's vision was one of decentralisation, not a prototype for what would become the WHO three decades later. Not that Davison did not see a use in that – because he did – but this was not the mission at hand here. Rather, his plan focused on the Red Cross movement. What he envisaged had to be located, developed and managed within the Red Cross world, not by state organisations. His vision was of a new organisation that would become an ally to Red Cross national societies, a generous co-ordinator that would share the latest medical knowledge and know-how that national societies would adapt to and implement in their local political, social, economic and religious contexts.[7] Davison, always the confident man in public, declared 'the beauty of this plan is that it conflicts with no one. It stimulates all good endeavour for general health'.[8]

Founding an International Health Organisation or a New Red Cross Player?

This overly broad organisation sometimes referred to as an 'international health organisation' or 'health bureau' by some delegates *versus* the new Red Cross organisation envisaged by Davison is perhaps one of the most interesting differences in conceptualising the future organisation that can be observed between the medical delegates and Davison. Some delegates envisioned a grand oracle of public health, with knowledge and science at the top, providing guidelines, norms and facts to the rest of the world, government and non-government stakeholders alike, and making recommendations on too wide an array of issues according to Davison.[9] One cannot help but wonder what would have happened had Davison given the delegates a completely free hand to shape the institution they wanted rather than to get them to approve the one he had already designed. Less than sixty years before, a handful of Genevan citizens had managed to get nation-states on board to create international conventions on the conduct of war. It is not unthinkable to imagine that prominent scientists assembled at Cannes could have – if given the chance and in the context of the rise of the expert as a figure of authority to design public policy[10] – succeeded in achieving a similar outcome: this time to create an international health organisation. Cannes can be understood as the foundational event for the League of Red Cross Societies just as it can be thought of as a missed opportunity that did not result in what would become the WHO thirty years later, after another world war. Success or missed opportunity, it is a matter of perspective, but certainly not of irresoluteness. Davison's plan was consciously more modest and therefore more realistic – a point he insisted on – and focused on the Red Cross movement exclusively and its volunteer, grassroots structure. It is clear that the way in which Davison conceptualised and envisaged the

League's work meant that the bulk of the work would be performed at the local level under the direction of Red Cross national societies, but with the support and coordination of a future League of Red Cross Societies. At no point did Davison present the League as an agency that would centralise and standardise global public health work whether within or beyond the Red Cross world. Rather, it would rely on local customs and local branches of Red Cross national societies. This method eventually filtered down in the Sections' work, such as the Child Welfare Section whose resolutions included that 'local health habits and racial customs, which are good, should be accepted and used as a foundation on which to build'.[11] This collaborative approach perhaps explains why the League of Red Cross Societies has endured since 1919. From its humble beginnings, it has always sought to support Red Cross Red Crescent national societies and facilitate their work rather than incorporate them in a centralised structure that would take decisions on their behalf or impose norms.[12] Davison's more modest ambition – in contrast with those of some delegates – seems to indicate that for him, a bird in the hand is worth two in the bush: better a small League of Red Cross Societies that could deliver on a delimited programme than a tentative 'international health organisation'. He had the means, support and experience to create a new player in the Red Cross world and that is what he did: no more, no less.

As Chairman of the American Red Cross War Council during the war, Davison understood that the strength of the Red Cross lay in the millions of volunteers, members and donors – not in a central organisation. The Red Cross only worked because it was popular and embodied in people across countries. In that sense, the Japanese and American Red Cross national societies were real successes, with a very large membership base, while older European national societies were more elitist, with a smaller membership base. One of Davison's main objectives for the future organisation that he had in mind became the creation of new national Red Cross societies to increase the Red Cross's membership base and therefore its means and its values in action. It is clear that for Davison there could exist the most central, medical, official organisation but if there was no popular support rooted in national societies and local branches of the Red Cross, such an organisation would become a dead letter. Davison was more focused on the individual and their work rather than on institutions, which might have been a trait of the country in which he grew up. Following his intervention to re-focus the work of the delegates, Davison further clarified the objective of the conference:

> we asked you to come here not to develop the organisation but to give us, not as national groups, your science. I do not know a Japanese from an American, or a Britisher from a Frenchman. It is the science you bring

to us. You put down what you believe is the best method of carrying the message to the peoples of the world, as to how to treat malaria, for example; you give that to our organization and our organization will carry the message.[13]

Davison insisted that operations remain focussed, saying that if the programme of work was too broad, the future League of Red Cross Societies would fail. He explained that 'the organization will have to be formed slowly, without restriction, without definitive lines. We have to mold to meet the situation'.[14] It should start with a realistic programme and expand if possible; his approach was that of a realist who considered resources in relation to aspirations. Following Davison's reframing, delegates were back on the tracks that had been laid for them and focussed on developing Davison's new organisation.

Creating the League of Red Cross Societies and Its Missions: The Dawn of a New Era for the Red Cross Movement

Throughout the conference, several names were proposed for the new institution, and those names reflect the conceptual work and imaginings of the delegates but also demonstrate that contrary to the consultative approach framing the conference, Davison already had a clear vision for the future League of Red Cross Societies. With regard to the name of the institution, the proceedings explained: 'The term *International Health Bureau* had been objected by some. The names *Central Health Bureau* and *Bureau of Health* had been suggested'.[15] The names *Red Cross International Council* and *Bureau of Hygiene and Public Health* were floated by Dr. Strong. Professor Calmette, the Assistant Director of the Pasteur Institute, noted that 'it would be wise to avoid giving to this bureau a title which would lead to any confusion with the *Office International d'Hygiène Publique*, already existing in Paris'.[16] Other names such as *Association Internationale des Croix-Rouges pour la lutte contre les Maladies Contagieuses* and *International Health Bureau* were proposed.[17] In fact, given that more than half a dozen potential names were used throughout the proceedings, an explanation is provided in one of their rare footnotes to explain that 'the organisation referred to in this memorandum under the name International Red Cross [yet another name] has become the League of Red Cross Societies'.[18]

The difficulty in naming this new organisation at the Cannes Medical Conference demonstrated the difficulty in conceptualising what it would be, what it would do, and to whom it would answer. What is interesting, however, is that the names that were candidly proposed by conference delegates focused on health and were headed towards a much larger programme of works than anticipated by Davison. As previously noted, some delegates envisioned an organisation like the later WHO, and this was not why Davison had called the meeting. While public health would be a central area of work for the future League of Red Cross Societies, it was not to be its sole purpose. The institution Davison had in mind was primarily a Red Cross institution: voluntary, transnational, neutral and democratic. The League of Red Cross Societies would be there to encourage the formation of Red Cross national societies around the world, develop the Junior Red Cross and act as a mailbox of the world but it certainly would not be a centralised global health organisation. While no name was formally agreed upon at Cannes, Davison already had views about what the new institution should be called and where it should be based. Colonel Strong, who was Professor of Medicine, Director of the Medical Research Department of the American Red Cross, US representative to the Interallied Sanitary Commission and a close ally to Davison, was Davison's voice through the conference. Colonel Strong 'referred to the question of title or name for the central organization which would probably be set up at the capital of the League of Nations, to carry on the activities of the *League of Red Cross Societies* in connection with the prevention of disease and the betterment of the health and general welfare of people'.[19] While conference meetings gave the impression to delegates that much was yet to be decided upon, some fundamentals (name, location, role, missions) were already very clear in Davison's mind. This was because he was shaping the new organisation to be a non-governmental humanitarian counterpart to his President's League of Nations.[20]

The Cannes Medical Conference also attempted to define the organisational structure and character of the future League of Red Cross Societies. For example, in his memorandum, Colonel Strong proposed an organisational chart for the new organisation that very much mirrored the division of work observed during the conference. He proposed that the following divisions be established within the new organisation: Information, Laboratory, Library, Museum, Publications, Sanitation, Miscellaneous Communicable Diseases, Vital Statistics, Tuberculosis, Industrial Hygiene, Venereal Diseases, Nursing and Child Welfare. The institution would be headed by a director aided by assistant directors supported by an executive committee of an international council of hygiene and public health, and national public health Red Cross representatives in each country. Strong's proposal also included other areas of work for the future League of Red Cross Societies that were not envisaged by Davison such as sewage, housing and water supply for example. Strong's proposed organisational chart (Chart 1) would form the basis for the one that the League operated under once

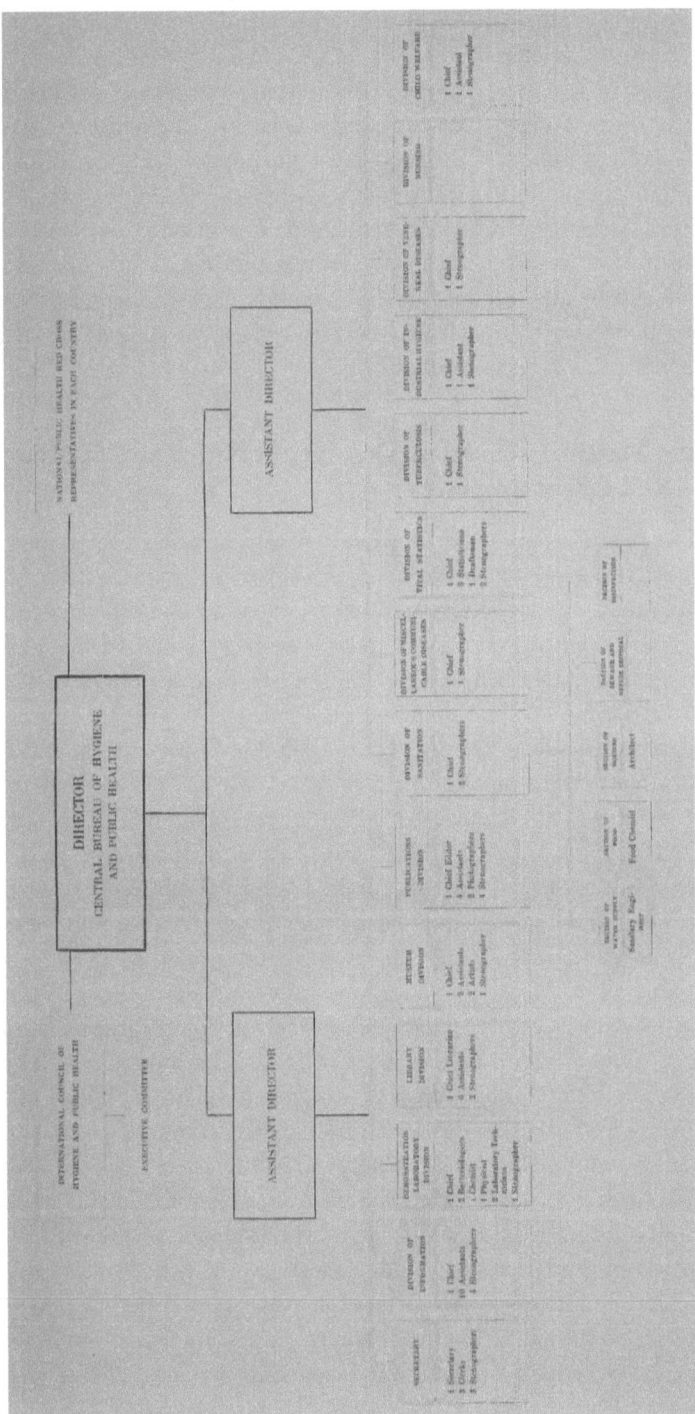

Chart 1 Professor Richard P. Strong's proposed organisational chart for the organisation to be born from the Cannes Medical Conference. The League's organisational chart would, in the fulness of time, include the Junior Red Cross Division and the Relief Section.

established.[21] Here again, what was drafted before Cannes in accordance with Davison's vision is what ended up being approved by Cannes delegates. Beyond the nature of the work of each division, it is interesting to note that Strong's proposal included a Museum and a Library. The Museum would serve to display equipment for educational purposes, while the Library would be equipped with a central bibliographical catalogue, that is a 'universal list of writings, books, and articles' on health and diseases.[22] The imagined institution would send the latest scientific information on disease and public health to all countries in different languages. This was a time when the circulation of research was heavily reliant on printed material, cataloguing and proactive dissemination.

Circulating Medical Knowledge: A Key Role for the Future League of Red Cross Societies

Strong, Davison and many other delegates firmly believed that access to information was the key to the betterment of world public health. They testified to a faith in science, information and education that was very much of the time. They had little doubt about the successes of science. In fact, global health issues appeared relatively easy to fix if one were to believe the general enthusiasm and optimism of the conference delegates. For them, the principal culprit was ignorance, and education was the solution. Time and time again, ignorance – rather than means, cultures, viruses or bacteria – was blamed for creating issues that would be fixed with educational propaganda. It was never envisioned that a key mission for the future League of Red Cross Societies would be to send legions of doctors to fight an epidemic outbreak. The primary mission of the League would be to educate and circulate information that would prevent the appearance or the spreading of diseases. To fight ignorance, many of the recommendations made by scientists at the conference pertained to education and 'propaganda'. French delegate Professor Roux spoke about a 'crusade' against disease, a word also used by British delegate Sir Arthur Newsholme,[23] while American delegate William H. Welch spoke of a 'gospel of health' that needed to be propagated throughout the world by the new institution.[24] American delegate Wickliffe Rose explained that 'public health work is about 90% education of the common man'.[25] A key recommendation from the Section on Preventive Medicine was that the new institution 'assemble and digest the public health laws and the sanitary codes of the important countries' to circulate what was deemed best practice in public health across the world.[26] This notion of 'important countries' hints at the prevalence of developed, imperial and hegemonic national societies in the League's early days.

Figure 2 Display of childhood welfare posters and propaganda at the Cannes Medical Conference.

Knowledge was to be the League's first weapon against diseases. At a time when many diseases could still not be cured through medications, avoiding contagion through appropriate hygiene and evidence-based best practices was of the utmost relevance. This is why all sections of the conference in one way or another recommended that the League of Red Cross Societies resort to 'propaganda literature' to educate people about good hygiene and public health and that in order to establish such literature it should promote the gathering and circulating of medical information (Figure 2). The League of Red Cross Societies became particularly active on that front as soon as it started its operations. Its *Bulletin* published information on the League's activities and that of national societies, but the League of Red Cross Societies also published its own public health monthly review titled *The World's Health*.[27] The review published copyright-free articles from medical practitioners so they could be widely circulated to Red Cross national societies and beyond. The free and wide dissemination of the latest medical research across the globe, of brochures, posters and educational films would become a major area of work for the League of Red Cross Societies from 1920 onward.

Notes

1 This was Davison's strong belief, and one only needs to look at the Paris Peace Conference, the profound divisions that emerged among the Allies, and the length of the process, to understand why Davison preferred doctors and scientists.
2 On this notion and its context, please refer to Mark Mazower, *Governing the World*, 94–115.
3 Hermann Biggs was then the Commissioner of Health for New York State, a Professor of Medicine, and was on the board of scientific directors for the Rockefeller Institute for Medical Research. 'Hermann M. Biggs', *Science* 58, no. 1508 (1923): 413–415. Richard Strong was Professor of Tropical Medicine at Harvard, Director of the Medical Research Department of the ARC and representative of the US to the Interallied Sanitary Commission in Paris. 'Obituary', *British Medical Journal*, 13 November 1948, 880. Strong is also known for having killed 13 people of the Bilibid Prison in Manila in an attempt to study strong reactions to cholera inoculation on 24 prisoners. Kristine A. Campbell, 'Knots in the Fabric: Richard Pearson Strong and the Bilibid Prison Vaccine Trials, 1905–1906', *Bulletin of the History of Medicine* 68, no. 4 (1994): 600–638. William H. Welch was President of the board of scientific directors of the Rockefeller Institute for Medical Research and Director of the School of Hygiene and Public Health at John Hopkins. Barry D. Silverman, 'William Henry Welch (1850–1934): the road to Johns Hopkins', *Baylor University Medical Center Proceedings* 24, no. 3 (2011): 236–242.
4 File 10, 'planning', in Z000363, IFRC archives, Geneva.
5 Davison, *Proceedings*, 46.
6 Ibid.
7 One of several areas in which the League would come to occupy this role is blood transfusion. See Jordan Evans, 'New Blood: The role of the League of Red Cross Societies in the development of blood transfusion services from 1946–1979', PhD dissertation, Flinders University, 2024.
8 Ibid.
9 Ibid, 47.
10 Rodogno *et al.*, *Shaping the transnational sphere*, 1. In the League of Nations' context, see Susan Pedersen, 'Back to the League of Nations', *The American Historical Review* 112, no. 4 (2007): 1110–1112.
11 Resolutions of the Section on Child Welfare, *Proceedings*, 105.
12 Melanie Oppenheimer, Susanne Schech, Romain Fathi, Neville Wylie and Rosemary Cresswell, 'Resilient Humanitarianism? Using Assemblage to re-evaluate the history of the League of Red Cross Societies', *The International History Review* 43, no. 3 (2021): 579–597.
13 Davison, *Proceedings*, 47.
14 Ibid, 48.
15 Strong, *Proceedings*, 176.
16 Calmette, *Proceedings*, 176. Albert Calmette was a student of Pasteur and became the codeveloper of the BCG vaccine against tuberculosis. Barbara J. Hawgood, 'Doctor Albert Calmette 1863–1933: founder of antivenomous serotherapy and of antituberculous BCG vaccination', *Toxicon* 37, no. 9 (1999):1241–1258.
17 Ibid.
18 *Proceedings*, 42.

19 Strong, *Proceedings*, 176.
20 This was a preoccupation for the ICRC that believed, initially at least, that Davison's plan went against the universality of the Red Cross movement. ICRC minutes, 26 February 1919.
21 This organisational chart was inserted between page 32 and 33 of the *Proceedings*. A comparison with that adopted by the League once in existence reveals some similarities, precisely because the organisational structure of the League and the health areas it would focus its work on had been drafted before Cannes and approved there. See the League's 1924 organisational chart in Daphne A. Reid and Patrick F. Gilbo, *Beyond Conflict. The International Federation of the Red Cross and Red Crescent Societies, 1919–1994* (Geneva: IFRC, 1997), 64.
22 Strong, *Proceedings*, 34.
23 Newsholme, *Proceedings*, 25.
24 Welch, *Proceedings*, 24.
25 Wickliffe Rose, *Proceedings*, 64.
26 Public Health Legislation, *Proceedings*, 142.
27 *Vers la Santé* (in French), *The World's Health* (in English) and *Por la Salud* (in Spanish) was published between 1922 and 1930. The monthly review is available at the IFRC in Geneva and is located on shelves B1320-B1321. Some issues have been digitised and are available on Gallica, the *Bibliothèque Nationale de France*'s digital library. Prior to this, *Vers la Santé* was preceded by the short-lived *International Journal of Public Health* (July 1920 to the end of 1921), cancelled because of financial difficulties. *The World's Health* and the League's *Information Bulletin* merged in 1931 under the name *Review and Information Bulletin*. Mélanie Blondin, Archivist, International Federation of Red Cross and Red Crescent Societies, email to author, 24 January 2023.

Chapter 5

DESIGNING THE ORGANISATIONAL STRUCTURE OF THE RED CROSS'S PEACETIME BODY

This final chapter considers how the Cannes Medical Conference set up the League of Red Cross Societies to be the Red Cross's peacetime body, with a focus on public health prevention, training and coordination for Red Cross activity across the world. Through further dissection of the work of conference delegates, it analyses how their proposed resolutions shaped the League's early activities in the 1920s, and the key prerogatives that the League of Red Cross Societies bestowed upon itself both to differentiate itself from the ICRC and to complement Red Cross national societies effectively. Instead of being reactive to conflict or preparing for conflict, the chapter argues that the League of Red Cross Societies proposed to diversify Red Cross activities to focus on the prevention of major public health issues of the time. This was a significant paradigm shift for the Red Cross Red Crescent movement. With regard to public health, prevention was judged to be far more effective and less costly than the task of curbing epidemics. Besides practical recommendations such as changes in legislation or direct support to certain populations, all working parties of the conference placed major importance on the circulation of knowledge. Chapter 5 outlines the workings and outcomes of the Cannes Medical Conference and how these transformed the Red Cross movement, proving a turning point towards a new phase of its existence.

The Seven Sections of the Cannes Medical Conference

Alongside plenary sessions where all conference delegates gathered, the Cannes Medical Conference ran seven working groups called 'sections', each working on a specific public health issue. The plenary sessions aimed to discuss the contours of the future Red Cross organisation Davison sought to establish: what it would do, its structure, its name and other fundamentals. Section work, however, focussed on specific topics. As explained in the previous chapter, these included malaria, venereal diseases, child welfare, tuberculosis, nursing, preventive medicine and publication, education and statistics. These sections were assembled to create an implementable programme of work for what became the League of Red Cross Societies. The way they functioned was straightforward. Each section met between plenary sessions across several days and was tasked to produce a report that contained resolutions that could be implemented or at least supported by the Red Cross Red Crescent movement. The smallest section, nursing, had 11 members, the malaria and venereal diseases sections had 12 members each, while the largest sections, preventive medicine and tuberculosis, had 22 members each. To be in a specific section, a delegate had to have direct expertise in the field. For instance, in the nursing section (Figure 3), most members were women with expertise and experience in nursing. Miss Julia C. Stimson was the Director of the Army Nurse Corps of the American Expeditionary Force, Miss A. Lloyd-Still the Matron of Nurses' Royal Infirmary, Miss Carrie M. Hall the Chief Nurse of the American Red Cross in France, Professor Emilia Malatesta Anselmi was the General Assistant to the General Inspector of the Italian Red Cross Nurses, Countess Nerina Gigliucci a volunteer nurse

Figure 3 Some of the women delegates to the Nursing section. From left to right: Miss Lloyd-Still, Miss Gill, Miss Stimson (Chair), Countess de Roussy de Sales, Professor Anselmi, Countess Gigliucci, Miss Hall.

in the Italian Red Cross, and Countess de Roussy de Sales was the Head Nurse of the *Société de Secours aux Blessés Militaires*. Grouping experts by fields ensured a degree of efficiency in the production of reports, as proceedings reveal no major disagreements over methods, treatments and resolution for specific diseases and health problems. The expertise assembled at Cannes was arranged in relation to the future organisational divisions of the League of Red Cross Societies. In other words, the programme of work for the League did not emerge at Cannes based on spontaneous discussions. Rather, experts (who often knew one another or one another's work) were selected in specific fields prior to the conference so that they could come up with a definite programme of work in areas that Richard P. Strong and Davison thought the future League of Red Cross Societies could be most helpful and successful.

The format of this book does not allow for the analysis of the work of each single section. The venereal diseases section is therefore used as an example for section work. Each section produced equally valuable reports which became the basis for the structural organisation and missions of the League of Red Cross Societies and the implementation of its early work throughout the 1920s. As of 2025, much remains to be explored with regard to the League's early work. The nursing division is the most documented to date, but there are equally large numbers of archival files on the League's work in the areas of malaria, tuberculosis and child welfare in the 1920s and 1930s available across archival repositories, at the IFRC's archives in Geneva, but also at the National Archives and Records Administration (NARA) in College Park, MD.[1] Undertaking such archival analyses would go a long way in understanding the League's operations, its contribution to the public health turn of the early twentieth century, and how it transformed the Red Cross movement from the inside.

The Venereal Diseases Section

Each of the seven sections of the Cannes Medical Conference produced its own report based on the group work of its members and preliminary outlines penned by Colonel Strong.[2] The one produced by the Venereal Diseases Section is typical of other reports published in the *Proceedings* and is worth analysing because it evidences that despite its benevolence, the Committee of Red Cross Societies defended and sought to maintain a political order that held a conservative, and at times patriarchal, understanding of the family.[3] The report approached venereal diseases holistically and made a wide range of recommendations, not only medical recommendations on treatment for example, but also social, cultural and legislative recommendations to tackle venereal diseases as a multifaceted problem, rather than a purely medical one.[4] This included encouraging early marriage and sex education, abolishing prostitution, and the provision of more entertainment and recreation.[5] The report of the venereal diseases section was nine pages long and proposed practical solutions to fight venereal diseases, containing much detail as to how this fight could be carried out and by whom. Given how venereal diseases plagued First World War armed forces, there was a moral panic at the time of the Cannes Medical Conference that demobilised soldiers would contaminate societies to which they were due to return. Much knowledge had been accumulated on venereal diseases during the war, and also about appropriate treatments. Besides medical recommendations that were more likely to be implemented by government-funded health services rather than the future League of Red Cross Societies, delegates identified what specific role the League could play with regard to venereal diseases. They concluded that primarily this role would revolve around educating people and getting the right information to them. By today's standards, this perhaps does not look like much but in the first decades of the twentieth century, this was essential work which would, in due course, be undertaken by the League of Red Cross Societies from its Geneva and then Paris office. Delegates recommended that the future organisation:

1. Assemble, classify and present to the national Red Cross societies the approved propaganda literature from the several nations which are active in this field.
2. Prepare suitable cinema films and adapt them in details and language to several countries.
3. Furnish the material for articles for newspapers, magazines, trade journals and other publications.
4. Provide posters illustrating in a popular way the salient facts relative to venereal diseases and the social hygiene movement.
5. Furnish satisfactory lecturers or experts who could attend important national conferences in countries where further progress requires the stimulation of such persons.[6]

Given that in 1919, no antibiotics existed to fully cure venereal diseases, treatments focussed on reducing the effects of symptoms. Education and prevention work were therefore the most effective tools to curb venereal disease infections globally by limiting contagion and the spread of the diseases. As a result, in the early 1920s, the League of Red Cross Societies did engage in all the above-mentioned venereal disease activities. The League released what was then referred to as 'propaganda' material in the form of literature, films and posters for circulation worldwide by numerous Red Cross national societies that requested them from the League. For example by 1921, within two years of its establishment, the League was able to loan 88 different films to Red Cross national societies. National Societies could and did request these reels on topics such as venereal diseases but also child welfare, tuberculosis, hygiene and the Junior Red Cross. Such educational movies were shown to hundreds of thousands of people across the world.[7] The League also created several pamphlets on venereal diseases, generally disseminated in five to six languages.[8] In 1921, the Venereal Diseases Division of the League issued an eight-page pamphlet titled *Venereal Diseases – Facts for Men and Women*.[9] By mid-1922, the League had produced four prospectuses and pamphlets on venereal diseases printed and circulated at nearly 50,000 copies.[10] Besides the first 25,000 copies produced by the League of its *Venereal Diseases – Facts for Men and Women*, the original templates of the publication were lent to the Belgian Red Cross for large reproduction, with the Russian Red Cross ordering a large number of them in Russian translation, and the Estonian and Latvian societies also planning a translation.[11] The brochure was so popular that it was revised in 1926. Earlier that year, the Report to the Secretary-General explained that 'numerous requests ha[d] been received, especially from the Latin-American countries, for the new edition of the League's brochure on venereal diseases'.[12] The revised brochure was published in English, Spanish, and French, but the League was happy to provide translations in other languages for orders above 5,000 copies.[13] Given that the brochures and pamphlets were likely circulated to many people through local branches of Red Cross national societies, they too, like the films, reached large numbers. National Societies clearly engaged with the League's public health programme on venereal diseases as it filled an important gap, notwithstanding that some of them were already doing such work before the League was created.[14]

The dissemination of medical knowledge through propaganda material was a direct recommendation that emerged from the Cannes Medical Conference. The success met by the League in that field led it to become a major leader in the global fight against venereal diseases in the interwar period. As part of the League's strategy to fight venereal diseases, it campaigned to unify national efforts against venereal diseases through a single international body. Given that national associations and organisations dealing with venereal diseases were not part of the Red Cross Red Crescent movement and that many of them pre-dated the creation of the League, the League was initially not best placed to fulfil this role. To remediate this position of latecomer and because it did not have the capacity to undertake the medical research that fed its publications, the League worked to become a global coordinator on venereal diseases work. To unite non-Red Cross venereal disease efforts with those of the Red Cross, the League campaigned for the creation and became a founding member of the International Union against Venereal Diseases (IUVD) in January 1923, officially known as the *Union Internationale Contre le Péril Vénérien*.

The founding story of the IUVD highlights that the multiple European conferences on venereal diseases organised or co-convened by the League in 1921 resulted in broad support for the establishment of a common plan to fight venereal diseases at a global level, and the League seized the opportunity to federate these energies. Within five years of the Cannes Medical Conference, the League established itself as a leading organisation for the discussion and tackling of venereal diseases worldwide. That it could encourage, organise and then support the creation of the IUVD in 1923 is in itself a testament to the credibility and acknowledgement of the League in that space. The practical support provided by the League to the IUVD – some funds, a space, secretariat support and a treasurer – enabled the IUVD to come into existence and become self-sustaining as its membership expanded.[15] In 1928, over 35 countries were represented within the Union, with over 50 member organisations, mostly national associations that combatted venereal diseases but also medical and government organisations, and Red Cross national societies. It is well beyond the scope of this chapter to study the history of the IUVD and its achievements. But testament to its legacy is the fact that it celebrated its hundredth anniversary in 2023 and is now known as the IUSTI, the International Union Against Sexually Transmitted Infections. Through the twentieth century, it has played a major role in encouraging, centralising and disseminating research on venereal diseases.[16] The role played by the League of Red Cross Societies in providing the impetus, resources and support that enabled the IUVD's creation remains little known, but its origins are indebted to the Cannes Medical Conference.[17]

While it is virtually impossible to quantify how many individuals benefited from education programmes and treatments provided by Red Cross national societies with the support of the League, the fact remains that the League took part in this global push towards better public health and that many national societies started venereal diseases work in the interwar period as a result of their association with the League, although a handful had started working in that space prior to the First World War.[18] This proactive – rather than reactive – approach to public health (education and preventive work) was one that certainly played a role in limiting the propagation of venereal diseases. It is impossible to estimate what would have happened in terms of global venereal disease infections had the League of Red Cross Societies not engaged in this work, meaning in turn that the level of success of the League's work is difficult to assess, as is often the case with humanitarian action. What is certain, however, is that the League of Red Cross Societies did engage in most of the activities proposed by reports of the Cannes Medical Conference's seven sections. All seven sections formed the League's DNA and, with the exception of Malaria, by 1924, they all remained either divisions, sections or bureaux in the League's organisational chart.[19] The fact that each of these seven sections resulted in an actual branch within the League of Red Cross Societies evidences that the League followed through with the recommendations made or approved at Cannes. This is because the Cannes Medical Conference was as much a gathering of experts to define actionable programmes of work as it was a validation of an organisational structure that had been envisioned before the conference to transform the Red Cross Red Crescent movement.

The Red Cross's Peacetime Body: Prevention, Training and Coordination

Across all seven sections of the conference there existed a guiding thread: a focus on education and knowledge that grounded future League of Red Cross Societies' actions into mostly preventive rather than curative work. Cannes' proceedings tell us that right from the beginning the League of Red Cross Societies was conceptualised as a proactive institution. Proceedings emphasised that the institution could very well be called upon in emergency situations but that its approach to its missions should primarily be proactive in order to avoid epidemics and calamities in the first place. Recommendations included that the new institution 'concentrate activities so far as possible on prevention rather than relief' and this was because results of prevention were said to be permanent rather than temporary as in the case of relief, and also because the cost of prevention was generally cheaper, increasing the effectiveness of humanitarian action.[20] This proactive character would not only be achieved through education and circulation of information but through the building up of the resilience and capacity of Red Cross national societies. The section on nursing was a clear example of this. Its report proposed that the future organisation host a nursing bureau that would act as 'an intelligence centre' on nursing and women's work in public health, 'undertake propaganda' in countries where nursing programmes are not well developed, "seek out in these countries [...] suitable personnel for training', and 'arrange conferences'.[21] The report further evidenced that much of this work could be undertaken using existing 'Red Cross assets' given that the war had resulted in the creation of many training centres and work opportunities for nurses, but also via creating opportunities such as scholarships. What the nurses of Cannes were particularly interested in was permanency, that is to say establishing a durable presence and training of nurses within each Red Cross national society to build resilience and operability. The League of Red Cross Societies would soon deliver on this aspiration through its own international public health nursing programme.[22]

This proactiveness at the core of the League's founding principles and which was much discussed at Cannes was a major shift for the Red Cross movement that had traditionally been a reactive body to events such as wars, although, of course, many international Red Cross conferences had aimed to anticipate and regulate future conflicts through a number of conventions. But essentially and primarily, the ICRC had been designed to prepare and react to wartime situations rather than attempting to prevent them. Not only did the League of Red Cross Societies propose an entire set of new missions for the Red Cross Red Crescent movement, but it also proposed a radical shift in approaching its activities. National societies would have to educate and prevent the eruption of emergencies rather than just responding to and preparing for them. There was a practical dimension to this method. American delegate and Commissioner of Health of the New York State Dr. Hermann Biggs, echoing others, explained that 'preventive work is so much more productive in return for money expended than is relief work'.[23] Medical experts knew that tackling an epidemic was far more costly and demanding than investing in the resources that would prevent it. The importance of preventive action was discussed across all seven sections of the Cannes Medical Conference. The Child Welfare section emphasised how 'preventable disabilities' could be avoided through good hygiene, visiting nurses to 'teach the mother' and education of good practices from an early age, such as care for the teeth. At this moment in time when the peace was under negotiation at Versailles, when reconstruction was a key agenda item for many nations, people spoke about the future, what it should look like and those who would build it: the children. Delegates of the Cannes Medical Conference unsurprisingly advocated for a 'world-wide child welfare campaign' as 'one of the most pressing needs of the day'.[24] As with other sections of the Cannes Medical Conference, child welfare would become an important area of work for the League of Red Cross Societies through the 1920s and beyond.[25]

Given the non-governmental nature of Davison's project, delegates often expressed that public health was 'a state function', 'a government function', but that 'where government agencies [did] not exist, it should be the purpose of voluntary agencies to stimulate the creation and the development of such agencies'.[26] Essentially, they saw the purpose of the future League of Red Cross Societies as one that would support government undertakings. It was not envisaged that the Red Cross would supplant any existing national health agency 'governmental or voluntary, but rather [that it] will aid them and help co-ordinate their activities'.[27] This idea of coordination at an international level of existing local and national efforts is absolutely central to the role that the delegates envisaged for the new organisation. Time and time again the words 'co-ordinate' and 'co-ordination' appear in the *Proceedings* of the Cannes Medical Conference. The future League of Red Cross Societies was conceptualised as a conductor of an orchestra where some degree of harmonisation would be created by the coordination of different organisations towards a precise goal in a precise situation in order to provide effective services and to avoid 'isolated and inefficient efforts'.[28]

Exploring section work at the Cannes Medical Conference enables us to draw several conclusions. First, the way in which the conference was structured around section work allowed for the production of implementable reports for the future League, with defined areas of work and methods to perform it. Second, the fact that all sections of the Cannes Medical Conference became divisions within the League once it was established a month after the conference demonstrates that Cannes served to both validate and further develop a programme of Red Cross work that had been envisioned prior to the conference, rather than the programme emerging autonomously as a result of the conference. Indeed, sections were defined ahead of the conference with delegates being invited on the basis that they had sufficient expertise to be assigned to a specific section. Expertise was triaged to make recommendations on specific diseases. Finally, and perhaps most importantly, Section reports provided at Cannes enable us to trace the League's DNA, as they provided a lasting road map for the League's interwar work, a work that profoundly altered the Red Cross Red Crescent movement and considerably expanded the range of its activities.

Notes

1 See for example: Melanie Oppenheimer, 'Nurses of the League: the League of Red Cross Societies and the development of public health nursing post-WWI', *History Australia* 17, no. 4 (2020): 628–644; Melanie Oppenheimer, 'Gender, personalities and the politics of humanitarianism: Nursing leaders of the League of Red Cross Societies between the wars' in *Humanitarianism, Empire and Transnationalism, 1760–1995* edited by Joy Damousi, Trevor Burnard and Alan Lester (Manchester: Manchester University Press, 2022), 241–263; Melanie Oppenheimer, Neville Wylie, Susanne Schech and Romain Fathi, with Jordan Evans, *The League of Red Cross Societies and Twentieth-Century Humanitarianism* (Cambridge: Cambridge University Press, forthcoming) and Annmarie Reid and Melanie Oppenheimer, 'Nurses of the League Mapping the international nurses of the League of Red Cross Societies who attended Bedford College, London', 2021 available at https://storymaps.arcgis.com/stories/689dd98c1 e32445d93d8fc7b4c1d2b83 [Accessed 25 August 2024].

2 File 10, 'planning', in Z000363, IFRC archives, Geneva.
3 Elisabeth Piller and Neville Wylie have noted that 'Great War-era humanitarianism was never a disinterested or impartial, let alone apolitical endeavour [...] [it also] became a means of implementing ideological agendas[...]'. Elisabeth Piller and Neville Wylie, *Humanitarianism and the Greater War 1914–1924*, 9.
4 Members of the Section on Venereal Diseases included Prof. Augusto Ducrey (who gave his name to the *Haemophilus ducreyi* bacteria that cause chancroid), William F. Snow, L. W. Harrison, F. N. Kay Menzies, Sir Arthur Newsholme, Dr. Milian, Dr. Emile Roux, Dr. T. Kabeshima, Dr. K. Nawa and Frederick F. Russell.
5 Interestingly, once operational the League soon realised that the diversity in national contexts made it difficult to propose universal social measures against VD and it soon focussed its work in that space on the circulation of medical information only, and the creation of material (brochures, films, posters) for members of the public on prevention and treatment of VD.
6 'Report of Section on Venereal Diseases', *Proceedings*, 94.
7 See for example: 'Films', 27 September 1921, page 1 and 2, box R510858696, subfile 'Health Seamen, Hygiene, Health, and Welfare of Seamen 1926 (Part 1 of 2)', IFRC archives, Geneva; *Information Circular* no. 14 (Paris: Ligue des Sociétés de la Croix-Rouge, 1923); *Bulletin d'Information* 7, no. 5 (Paris: Ligue des Sociétés de la Croix-Rouge, 1928); 162 and *Bulletin d'Information* 4, no. 7 (Paris: Ligue des Sociétés de la Croix-Rouge, 1925): 153. Films were a common and effective way of circulating medical information in this period. Christian Bonah and Anja Laukötter, 'Screening Diseases. Films on Sex Hygiene in Germany and France in the First Half of the 20th Century', *Gesnerus* 72, no. 1 (2015): 5–14.
8 *Information circular* no. 6 (Paris: The League of Red Cross Societies, 1922),12, box R510858696, IFRC archives, Geneva.
9 *Information circular* no. 19 (Paris: The League of Red Cross Societies, 1921), 10, box R510858696, IFRC archives, Geneva.
10 *Information circular* no. 6 (Paris: The League of Red Cross Societies, 1922), 13, box R510858696, IFRC archives, Geneva.
11 Ibid.
12 'Report of the Secretary General of the League of Red Cross Societies to the Board of Governors 1926', 23 in RG P78 box 30, NARA, College Park (MD).
13 *Bulletin d'Information* 5, no. 12 (Paris: Ligue des Sociétés de la Croix-Rouge, 1926): 401–402.
14 Walter Clarke, 'Venereal Diseases. A Challenge to the Red Cross', *Bulletin of the League of Red Cross Societies*, 2, no. 4–5 (Paris: League of Red Cross Society, 1921): 176–184.
15 Claude H. Hill, 'The League of Red Cross Societies', *Bulletin of the Pan American Union*, 57, no. 4 (1923): 326.
16 This role is yet to be documented by historians as limited research has been published on the IUVD and how the League contributed to its creation. Theodore J. Bauer, 'Half a Century of International Control of the Venereal Diseases.' *Public Health Reports (1896–1970)*, 68, no. 8 (1953): 779–787; Thorstein Guthe, 'The International Union against the Venereal Diseases and the Treponematoses and the World Health Organisation', *The British Journal of Venereal Diseases*, 36, no. 1 (1960): 4–6.
17 For a more comprehensive history of the League's work on venereal diseases, please refer to chapter 4 in Melanie Oppenheimer, Neville Wylie, Susanne Schech and Romain Fathi, with Jordan Evans, *The League of Red Cross Societies and Twentieth-Century Humanitarianism*.

18 In the interwar period, such national societies include but are not limited to those of Germany, Argentina, Belgium, Cuba, Spain, France, the USSR, India, Italy, Japan, Latvia, Norway, New-Zealand, Poland, Sweden, Switzerland, Czechoslovakia, South Africa, Romania, Columbia, Finland, Siam, Venezuela and Belgian Congo. *Bulletin de la Ligue des Sociétés de la Croix-Rouge* 14, no. 8 (Paris: Ligue des Sociétés de la Croix-Rouge, 1933), 157.
19 See the chart published in Reid and Gilbo, *Beyond Conflict*, 64.
20 See page 147 and 42 of the *Proceedings*.
21 'Report of the Section on Nursing', *Proceedings*, 137.
22 Melanie Oppenheimer, 'Nurses of the League', 628–644.
23 Hermann Biggs, *Proceedings*, 42.
24 Report on Child Welfare, *Proceedings*, 98–102. The fate of children, in particular those of Germany and Austria-Hungary initially, motivated activists such as Eglantyne Jebb to establish the Save the Children Fund earlier that year. The work of the fund would soon expand across Europe and the world. Linda Mahood, *Feminism and Voluntary Action: Eglantyne Jebb and Save the Children, 1876–1928* (Basingstoke: Palgrave Macmillan, 2009), 142–184. See also Emily Baughan, *Saving the Children. Humanitarianism, Internationalism, and Empire* (Berkeley: University of California Press, 2021), 18–77.
25 See the multiple examples of child welfare work conducted by the League of Red Cross Societies and discussed in Daphne A. Reid and Patrick F. Gilbo, *Beyond Conflict*, 42–82.
26 Wickliffe Rose, 54.
27 Welch, *Proceedings*, 51.
28 Strong, *Proceedings*, 32.

CONCLUSION

In 1996 historian John F. Hutchinson noted that '[t]he Cannes conference did exactly what Davison wanted: it put the scientific stamp of approval on his vision of the future' of the Red Cross Red Crescent movement.[1] Immediately after the conference, Davison cabled that the 'conference closed under conditions which are almost thrilling as manifestations of appreciation and approval of programme have gone quite beyond my fondest hope – resolutions passed will frame foundation for world work which I have no hesitation in predicting will become historical'.[2] If success is assessed in relation to the goals of those who organised and supported the conference – key among them Henry P. Davison, William P. Strong and Woodrow Wilson from a distance – Cannes was a resounding success. Davison's plan for a new organisation in the Red Cross world focussing on the betterment of public health was met with enthusiasm by leading scientific and medical figures of the time, and it was subsequently approved and birthed by five prominent Red Cross national societies who gathered at Hotel Regina, in Paris, on 5 May 1919. Conference delegates fully supported Davison's intuition that while the war was over, staff and goodwill for the Red Cross should not be lost to demobilisation but redeployed towards public health. Delegates concluded that 'no other organisation is so well prepared to undertake these great responsibilities at the present time as the Red Cross, and no movement better deserves the hearty and enthusiastic support of all people than does this'.[3] This vision, however, required a significant shift in mentality within the Red Cross movement, a step that the ICRC was not interested in taking, preferring instead to focus on wartime humanitarianism, international law and post-war reconstruction, thus remaining true to its historical roots. Scientific approval, the ICRC's reluctance to embrace peacetime public health work, and an article in the Covenant of the League of Nations provided a rationale, space and mandate for the creation of the League of Red Cross Societies. Davison provided the energy and leadership, and the American Red Cross, the money. He travelled extensively across Europe prior to the conference, made useful connections and proposed a mature project that delegates of the Cannes Medical

Conference transmuted into practical recommendations. Most importantly perhaps, Davison worked hard to get public opinion on his side, something that took the ICRC by surprise.

Historian Julia Irwin has shown how 'publicity' and 'propaganda' were used by the American Red Cross, not only to gain support from the population but also to further expand its activities. Davison was a central player in the American Red Cross' publicity turn during the First World War.[4] Predictably, he resorted to similar methods to secure broad support for the future League of Red Cross Societies through copious paid advertising in the months between February and May 1919, when the League of Red Cross Societies was being created. Davison also actively promoted the conference as it was happening, sending glowing reports to the press explaining that 'delegates [were] working night and day' because of the 'urgency and importance' of the subject matter.[5] Reports he circulated to the press were very optimistic about scientists' abilities to cure the world's health problems and all led to the same conclusion: that the organisation he had in mind was needed, justified and could be 'functioning within a few weeks'.[6] Being talked about and presented in a good light buoyed up stakeholders in supporting what appeared to be a successful endeavour thanks to the self-fulfilling prophecy of mass communication. Cable correspondence between Davison's closest American and British supporters during the conference, together with financial statements of the Cannes Medical Conference, both attest to Davison's strategic use of the press to promote the event and secure positive public sentiment.[7] Reports on the conference, and sometimes Davison's own verbatim quotes that he sent to the press, were published in American, British, French, Belgian and Italian newspapers. From a business point of view, Cannes both justified and created a need for the future League of Red Cross Societies, which made Davison's endeavour undeniable. As noted by the former Henry Dunant Society's President, Roger Durand, Davison's publicity campaign did not finish with the conference. Within months, key recommendations and reports from sections were published in four languages through the League's *Bulletin*, through the publication and dissemination of the *Proceedings* of the conference, and of a beautifully crafted illustrated record of the conference.[8]

However, Davison's business-like methods, Wilson's support, and financial resources drawn from the American Red Cross cannot alone explain why the ideas behind the League of Red Cross Societies became so popular among scientists, the leadership of some Red Cross national societies, politicians and the public. At many levels, the Cannes Medical Conference ushered in the dawn of a new era for the Red Cross Red Crescent movement. The seeds of that new era, however, had long been germinating, with the First

World War accelerating their development. Cannes and the League of Red Cross Societies represented a crystallisation of ideas and attitudes about the future of the Red Cross Red Crescent movement. This crystallisation needed precipitation during what Davison called 'the psychological moment', which he had the vision and means to seize between the Armistice and the Treaty of Versailles.[9]

On 22 April 1919, within a fortnight of the closing of the Cannes Medical Conference, the ICRC was advised that statutes were being drafted for a League of Red Cross Societies. The ICRC was informed that the League would be a separate organisation that would be tasked with implementing the medical recommendations made at Cannes and that it would be ratified officially on 5 May 1919 in Paris. Importantly, it was made clear to the ICRC that the new League would, in the fullness of time, be opened up to yesterday's enemies.[10] During the formation of the League, ICRC representatives William Rappard and Renée-Marguerite Cramer were sent to Paris to follow these new developments. They were also there to prevent the constitution of a 'hostile or even exclusive' institution while preserving as close a relationship as possible without endangering what the ICRC held as the fundamental principles of the Red Cross.[11] The ICRC was supportive of the creation of the League of Red Cross Societies providing it would not become partisan and that it would not challenge ICRC primacy within the movement. Between January and May 1919, the ICRC received constant assurances from Davison in that direction. The ICRC recognised that it could not prevent the League's creation but regretted 'la méthode peu démocratique' (the not very / barely democratic method) through which the League was founded, and the fact that it did not respect the 'universal and impartial character' of the Red Cross.[12] Despite its reservations, the ICRC agreed to collaborate with the League because it was convinced that this state of affairs was temporary and that the League would grow to become more international, which it did through the 1920s.[13] Immediately after its foundation, the League of Red Cross Societies sent a delegation to Geneva on 12 May 1919 to once again reassure the ICRC that the League's vocation was indeed to become universal. In the early months of the League's foundation, official communications between both institutions were courteous, even encouraging.[14]

This courteous relationship, however, did not last, as the ICRC and the League of Red Cross Societies spent most of the 1920s trying to find a way to work together amid competition and at times suspicion between the two organisations. In 1928, after lengthy negotiations, the two organisations alongside national societies formalised and defined what they referred to as the International Red Cross.[15] The first statutes of the International Red Cross recognised the independence of the League of Red Cross Societies, the

ICRC, and the national societies, providing them with a framework within which to work with one another. Although the League and the ICRC timidly collaborated on a range of initiatives in the interwar period, the Second World War prompted them to become more cooperative with one another. Subsequently, both institutions have coexisted in Geneva and continue to work together, each with their areas of expertise. What was at times perceived as a schism within the movement, or a mild opposition in 1919 and throughout the 1920s, has, on the whole, developed to the advantage of a Red Cross movement which is now much larger, stronger and diverse, and therefore relevant across local, national and international contexts.

A more direct challenge to the League in the early 1920s was, perhaps, the receding tide of Wilsonianism. The US Senate blocked the country's entry into the League of Nations – an organisation Wilson fought so hard to get up – whilst Democratic party nominee James M. Cox (and Wilson's successor) lost the 1920 American presidential election to Republican Warren G. Harding, further curtailing past US international ambitions and closing the chapter of the long Wilson presidency. A similar withdrawal from world affairs took place within the American Red Cross which provided the League with the vast majority of its funding in its early years. Davison spent the last years of his life resisting the American Red Cross's trend to diminish its financial support towards the League. As opposed to Wilson, however, Davison's less expansive ambitions succeeded in the long run. While the League's budget was frail in its early years, the League endured and progressively flourished. Key leadership roles in the League, together with funding, continued to come from the United States, albeit more modestly, and European Red Cross National Societies gradually strengthened their involvement in the League during the interwar period. Subsequently, Scandinavian national societies and national societies of formerly colonised countries became central to League operations in the decades that followed the Second World War. The United States, through the American Red Cross, has remained an active member of the League ever since its foundation. The increased involvement of other Red Cross Red Crescent Societies in the League, be that through leadership positions, programs, and funding, in many ways vindicated Davison's vision.

With the foundation of the League of Red Cross Societies, public health work in the Red Cross movement became institutionalised and globalised, and this was made possible through the work of the Cannes Medical Conference delegates. While some Red Cross national societies had ventured into public health since the late nineteenth century, the League's creation saw peacetime and public health work encouraged and developed across the entire movement. While the League of Red Cross Societies formalised and accelerated a trend that preceded its creation, it nonetheless renewed the tenets of the Red

Cross Red Crescent movement at the international level. It broadened the movement's focus on wartime and war-related work to encompass peacetime work. It was proactive in seeking to improve global public health and limit the spread of diseases, rather than being exclusively focussed on situations of conflict.[16] The League focused on the local by stimulating the creation of Red Cross national societies and working with local branches rather than seeking to centralise the Red Cross movement. During the 1920s and beyond, the League of Red Cross Societies prioritised delivering on the programme of work established at Cannes, the skeleton of which was shaped by Henry P. Davison, fleshed out by his ally Richard P. Strong, and fully developed through the interactions of the medical staff assembled at the conference. In that, the *Proceedings* of this conference represent a real and practical manifesto for the League of Red Cross Societies; they provided it with specific tasks and areas of work. It was not imposed by states, politicians or Red Cross leadership, but conceived collaboratively by medical specialists. Without such a manifesto, the League of Red Cross Societies may not have taken off or may have erred for years in attempting to define its mission. Cannes enabled the future League to carve out an operational space within the Red Cross world and in that it represents a landmark event in the history of the Red Cross Red Crescent movement. Although assessing the work of the League of Red Cross Societies in the 1920s is beyond the scope of this book, it is clear that the major resolutions of the conference provided a roadmap for the League's work. As per the conference's recommendations, the newly minted League of Red Cross Societies created divisions and sections that mirrored those of the Cannes Medical Conference, although some took prominence over others, such as the Nursing Division that became larger than the Venereal Diseases Section, while other services were added, such as the Junior Red Cross Division, another major division for the League of Red Cross Societies in the 1920s. Those divisions and the sections within them spent much of the interwar period implementing in practical ways recommendations that can be traced to the Cannes Medical Conference and its proceedings. That work, however, is yet to be fully analysed in the historiography.[17]

The Cannes Medical Conference and the creation of the League of Red Cross Societies form part of a greater medical and public health ecosystem they contributed to strengthen. From the mid-nineteenth century onwards, public health became integral to state prerogatives and apparatuses with a focus on the national and imperial frameworks. The organising of regular international medical conferences, and the creation of the *Office International d'Hygiène Publique* in 1907 in particular, alongside that of the International Health Commission of the Rockefeller Foundation in 1913, signalled a move beyond these frameworks to address public health at a global level. Although the foundation of the League of Red Cross Societies preceded the creation of the Health Committee of the League of Nations, later to become to League of Nations Health Organisation, and that of other international organisations and international unions (for the blind, against tuberculosis, against venereal diseases etc.), it belongs to the great moment of internationalisms born out of the ashes of the First World War. The conflict's scale, intensity and global repercussions made many aware of the integrated nature of the world in the twentieth century. Public health was one of several areas where state and voluntary organisations alike, alongside medical professionals and volunteers, seized the opportunity of peace to create international structures to improve the world's health beyond states' borders and racial, economic and religious distinctions. These new structures soon started to collaborate with one another.[18]

The full extent of the League's relationships with international organisations in the interwar period is yet to be fully documented. Considerable archival materials exist to undertake this research. Although the International Labour Organisation and the League of Nations Health Organisation were created and funded by governments and the League of Red Cross Societies was not, and although their missions and aims greatly differed, there were many overlapping spaces for collaboration on specific diseases and programs. As early as 1922, a resolution of the newly formed Health Committee of the League of Nations explained that the League of Red Cross Societies focused on 'popular instructions in matters of health' and that both organisations agreed to a 'mutual exchange of their documents and proposals' in such matters.[19] The League became a technical advisor to multiple international organisations, while representatives of the latter were often associated with the League, formally or not. In fact, a prosopography of the people involved in global public health in the 1920s would evidence interconnectedness among this cohort of people who often moved from one organisation to the other.[20] From an institutional perspective, these connections – be they of a private, professional or organisational nature – advanced the League's agenda and prestige within the Red Cross movement. From its inception, the League was decisively outward-looking. Its missions were primarily anchored within the Red Cross world but in order to achieve them, the League's leadership worked to secure a seat at the table of a number of international organisations, be that as observer, advisor, or member.

On the whole, the Cannes Medical Conference openly signalled the public health turn of the Red Cross Red Crescent movement. It was both a performative and radical event. Performative because the delegates' reputation was used to justify the foundation of the League when much of its organisational structure and missions had been locked in before the conference. Despite this, it was a radical event for the Red Cross Red Crescent movement. Cannes capitalised on the experiences of some national societies that had started to invest the public health and disaster management fields prior to the First World War and convincingly proposed to make such areas of work integral to the Red Cross Red Crescent movement. Cannes established a viable programme of work that considerably expanded the movement's missions and prerogatives in the interwar period. It also altered the balance of power within the movement. The ICRC's ascendency was challenged. Cannes led to a League of Red Cross Societies that established a federated governance model for the Red Cross, with each national society having a voice and a vote to turn the movement towards directions it supported, whereas the ICRC was exclusively composed of co-opted Genevan citizens. In a way, this trademark had underpinned some of its successes thanks to the core concept of neutrality, but it also had limitations. The federated model proposed by the League unleashed a powerful energy that saw national societies emboldened to pursue new roles within their national – and at times imperial – contexts, generating some degree of amiable competitive spirit between national societies, breathing new life into the movement.

Notes

1 Hutchinson, *Champions of Charity*, 299.
2 Cable from Davison, 1919, 'Cannes Conference – Copy from Hoover Institution Archives', Folder 8, Box Z000355, IFRC archives, Geneva. The date, barely legible on the cable is most certainly 12 April 1919, one day after the end of the conference. It is not clear to whom the cable is addressed either but other cables in this file were sent to Colonel Robert E. Olds (American Red Cross Commissioner in Europe), Colonel Ernest Bicknell (Vice-Chairman of the American Red Cross and future Secretary General of the League), Stockton Axson (National Secretary of the American Red Cross) and also Otis Cutler (future Acting Chairman of the League's Board of Governors).
3 'Recommendations and Resolutions of the Conference', *Proceedings*, 12.
4 Julia Irwin, *Making the World Safe*, 68–69 and 79–93.
5 Davison to Marshall, 5 April 1919, 'League of Red Cross Societies Miscellaneous records', Box 1, Folder 8, Hoover Institution Library & Archives.
6 Ibid.
7 'League of Red Cross Societies Miscellaneous records, Financial Statements', Box 1, Folder 15, Hoover Institution Library & Archives.
8 Durand, *La Conférence Médicale de Cannes*, 65.
9 Davison, *Proceedings*, 22.
10 ICRC minutes, 22 April 1919.
11 ICRC minutes, 23 April 1919.
12 ICRC minutes, 5 May 1919.
13 By 1924, the League had 51 member national societies spread across the world. By order of admission to the League, they are the Red Cross or Red Crescent national

societies of: France, Italy, Japan, United Kingdom, United States of America, Belgium, Norway, Portugal, Brazil, Australia, Peru, Canada, Argentina, South Africa, Greece, Sweden, New Zealand, Denmark, Romania, Venezuela, Cuba, China, India, Netherlands, Spain, Serbia, Poland, Switzerland, Czechoslovakia, Uruguay, Chile, Thailand, Austria, Finland, Hungary, Bulgaria, Luxembourg, Estonia, Paraguay, Colombia, Costa Rica, Germany, Ecuador, Danzig, Bolivia, Latvia, Albania, Guatemala, Mexico, Netherlands East Indies and Lithuania.

14 ICRC, '182me circulaire', 20 May 1919.
15 David P. Forsythe, 'The International Red Cross: Decentralization and its Effects', *Human Rights Quarterly*, 40, 1 (2018): 74.
16 This radical change was central to Davison's project. When discussing the missions of the League of Red Cross Societies, he explained: 'the conception involves not alone efforts to relieve human suffering, but to prevent it'. *Statement of Henry P. Davison, Chairman, on the behalf of the American Red Cross War Council on its retirement, March 1, 1919*, The American Red Cross, National Headquarters, Washington DC, 1919, 7.
17 Some of that work will be explored in a book on the League of Red Cross Societies to be published in 2026: Melanie Oppenheimer, Neville Wylie, Susanne Schech and Romain Fathi, with Jordan Evans, *The League of Red Cross Societies and Twentieth-Century Humanitarianism* (Cambridge: Cambridge University Press, forthcoming).
18 Iris Borowy, *Coming to Terms with World Health. The League of Nations Health Organisation 1921–1946* (Frankfurt am Main: Peter Lang, 2009), 41–76, 140 and 180.
19 Health Committee of the League of Nations, 1922 in file R816/12B/8138/8138, UN Archives, Geneva.
20 Examples include Léon Bernard, Albert Calmette and Hugh S. Cumming, delegates at the Cannes Medical Conference and later members of the Health Committee of the League of Nations, as well as René Sand who became Secretary General of the League of Red Cross Societies. Martin David Dubin, 'The League of Nations Health Organisation' in *International Health Organisations and Movements, 1918–1939*, ed. Paul Weindling (Cambridge: Cambridge University Press, 1995), 60–64; *Monthly Summary of the League of Nations January 1926*, vol. 6 no. 1, 15 February 1926, 30.

APPENDIX

List of Delegates at the Cannes Medical Conference

The order of presentation and the acronyms appear as reported in the *Proceedings* published by the League of Red Cross Societies in 1919.[1]

Great Britain

S. Lyle Cummins, Colonel, C. M. G., A. M. S., Adviser in Pathology, British Armies in France; Professor of Pathology, R. A. M. P. College, London.

L. W. Harrison, Brevet Colonel, R. A. M. C., D. S. O., K. H. P., Lecturer in Venereal Diseases, Military Hospital, Rochester Row; Adviser in Venereal Diseases, Army Medical Department, London, S.W.

Edward C. Hort, F. R. C. P., Edinburgh, Hon. Lt. Colonel, R. A. M. C., Late Director of Bacteriological Laboratory, Addington Park Enteric Hospital.

Dr. Henry Kenwood, C. M. G., D. P. H., F. R. S. E., Professor of Hygiene and Public Health with the University of London: President of Soc. of Med. Officers of Health of Great Britain; Medical Officer of Health for County of Bedfordshire, England.

Truby King, C. M. G., M. B., B Sc., (Public Health) Edinburgh, Lecturer on Mental Diseases at University of Otago (N. Z.): General President, Royal New Zealand Society for the Health of Women and Children.

Sir John Lumsden, K. B. E., M. D., Vice Chairman and Director-in-Chief, Joint War Committee of B. R. C. S. and Order of St. John in Ireland; Senior Physician, Mercer's Hospital, Dublin.

N. Kay Menzies, M. D., F. R. C. P. E., D. P. H., etc., Principal Assistant Medical Officer. Public Health Department, London County Council.

Sir Arthur Newsholme, K. C. B., M. D., Fellow and Milroy Lecturer of the Royal College of Physicians; Late Principal Medical Officer of the Local Government Board; Member of Council of the Imperial Cancer Research Fund, etc.

Sir Robert W. Philip. Hon. Lt. Colonel. R. A. M. C., President of the Royal College of Physicians of Edinburgh; Professor of Tuberculosis and Clinical Medicine, University of Edinburgh.

Sir Ronald Ross. K. C. B. K. C. M. G., F. R. S., Nobel Laureate, Colonel, Army Medical Service, Consultant in Malaria, War Office. London.

France

Dr. P. Armand-Delille, Physician to the Paris Hospitals: General Secretary of the 'Oeuvre Grancher'.

Dr. Léon Bernard, Professor in the Faculty of Medicine, Paris; Physician to the Laënnec Hospital, Paris.

Prof. Albert Calmette. Assistant Director of the Pasteur Institute, Paris; Member of the Academy of Medicine; Correspondent of the Academy of Sciences; Director of the Pasteur Institute, Lille.

Prof. Paul Courmont, Professor of Hygiene in the Faculty of Medicine; Director of the Bacteriological Institute, Lyon.

Dr. A. Laveran, Member of the Academy of Science.

Dr. Milian, Physician to the Hospital St. Louis, Paris.

Dr. Maurice Péhu, Physician to the « Hôpital de la Charité », Lyon.

Prof. Adolphe Pinard, Honorary Professor in the Faculty of Medicine, Paris; Member of the Academy of Medicine.

Dr. Edouard Rist, Physician to the Laënnec Hospital, Paris.

Dr. Emile Roux (Chairman of the Conference), Director of the Pasteur Institute, Paris; Member of the Institute of France and the Academy of Medicine.

Prof. Fernand Vidal, Professor in the Faculty of Medicine, Paris; Member of the Academy of Medicine.

Italy

Dr. Prof. Cesare Baduel, Professor of Pathology and Clinical Medicine in the Faculty of Medicine of the Superior Institute, Florence; Physician to the Hospital Santa Maria Novella, Florence; Chief Medical Inspector and Chief of The Bureau of Sanitary and Social Welfare of the Italian Red Cross, Rome.

Prof. Dr. Giuseppe Bastianelli, Lt. Colonel, Italian Army M. C., Physician and Pathologist, Polyclinic Hospital, Rome.

Prof. Aldo Castellani, Lt. Colonel, Royal Italian Medical Service (Naval Branch), Emeritus Professor of Tropical Medicine, Colombo Medical School.

Prof. Augusto Ducrey, Director of the 'Clinica Dermosifilopatica' of the University of Genoa.

Prof. Dr. Camillo Golgi, Senator, Professor of Pathology at the University of Pavia; President of the Superior Council of Public Health.
Prof. Dr. B. Gosio, Prof. of Bacteriology, University of Rome; Chief of the Bacteriological Laboratory of the Italian Board of Health.
Prof. Edoardo Maragliano, Senator, Director of the Medical Clinic of the University of Genoa; War Department Inspector for the Prevention of Tuberculosis in the Italian Army.
Dr. Ettore Marchiafava, Senator, Prof. at the University of Rome; Vice-President of the Italian Red Cross.
Dr. Prof. Camillo Poli, Professor at the University of Genoa; President of the Society. For the Prevention of Tuberculosis, Genoa; Delegate of the Italian Red Cross for Sanitary and Social Welfare in the Province of Genoa.
Dr. Prof. Francesco Valagussa, Professor of Pediatrics at The University of Rome; Chief Physician to the Hospital Bambino Gesù; Delegate of the Italian Pediatric Society to the Italian Red Cross; Lt. Colonel, Medical Department, Italian Red Cross, Rome.

Japan

Dr. T. Kabeshima, Principal Physician to the Japanese Navy.
Dr. K. Nawa, Japanese Army Medical Service.

United States

Chandler P. Anderson, Counsellor of the Committee of Red Cross Societies.
Edward R. Baldwin, M. D., (Hon) M. A., Director of the Edward L. Trudeau Foundation and Trudeau School of Tuberculosis; Editor-in-Chief of American Review of Tuberculosis, Saranac Lake, N. Y.
Hermann M. Biggs, A. B., M. D., LL. D., Commissioner of Health, New York State; Professor of Medicine, New York University; Member, Board of Scientific Directors, Rockefeller Institute for Medical Research; Member, International Health Board, Rockefeller Foundation.
Hugh S. Cumming, M. D., Assistant Surgeon General, U. S. Public Health Service; Sanitary Supervisor of Service Activities in Europe.
Livingston Farrand, A. B., M. D., LL. D., Chairman, Central Committee, American Red Cross. Washington D. C.
Albert H. Garvin, M. D., Chief, Bureau of Tuberculosis, A. R. C. Commission to France; Supt., New York Sanitorium for Tuberculosis, Ray Brook, N. Y.
Samuel McClintock Hamill, M. D., Professor, Diseases of Children, Post Graduate Department, University of Pennsylvania; Director of Child Welfare for the State of Pennsylvania, Philadelphia, PA.

L. Emmett Holt, A. B., M. D., LL. D., Professor, Diseases of Children, Columbia University, New York; Member of the Board of Scientific Directors of the Rockefeller Institute for Medical Research; Physician-in-Chief to the Babies' Hospital, New York.

William Palmer Lucas, A. B., M. D., Professor of Pediatrics, University of California Medical School; Physician in Charge of Children's Service, University Hospital, San Francisco, California; Chief of the Children's Bureau, American Red Cross in France.

Henry Morgenthau, Former United States Ambassador to Turkey.

Wickliffe Rose, A. B., A. M., LL. D., General Director of the International Health Board of the Rockefeller Foundation.

Frederick F. Russell, M. D., Sc. D. Colonel, M. C., U. S. A., Professor of Pathology and Tropical Medicine. Army Medical College, Washington, D. C.; Chief of the Division of Infectious Diseases and Laboratories, Surgeon General's Office, War Department, Washington, D. C.

William F. Snow, A. B., M. A., M. D., Lieutenant Colonel, M. C., U. S. A., Professor, Hygiene and Public Health, Leland Stanford Jr. University; General Secretary, American Social Hygiene Association; Chairman, Executive Committee, United States Interdepartmental Social Hygiene Board.

Richard P. Strong, Ph. B., M. D., Sc. D., Colonel, M. C., U. S. A., Professor Tropical Medicine, Harvard University Medical School; Director, Medical Research Department, A. R. C.; Representative from the United States to the Interallied Sanitary Commission, Paris.

Fritz B. Talbot, A. B., M. D., Instructor in Pediatrics, Harvard Medical School; Chief, Children's Medical Department, Massachusetts General Hospital; Member of Committee for Conservation of Child Life to Massachusetts State Board of Health.

Lillian D. Wald, Founder and Head Resident, Henry Street Settlement, New York; Representative of Federal Children's Bureau of Department of Labor, U.S.A.

William H. Welch, A. B., M. D., LL. D., Director of the School of Hygiene and Public Health, Johns Hopkins University, Baltimore MD.; President of the Board of Scientific Directors of the Rockefeller Institute for Medical Research.

William Charles White, M. D., Medical Director, Tuberculosis League, Pittsburgh, PA.; Director of Tuberculosis Unit to Italy, American Red Cross; Former Chief of Bureau of Tuberculosis, American Red Cross, France; Member of Executive Committee, American National Tuberculosis Association.

Linsly R. Williams, A. M., M. D., Lt. Col., M. C., U. S. A., Director, Commission for the Prevention of Tuberculosis in France, International Health Board.

APPENDIX   81

Delegates to the Nursing Section

Great Britain

Miss A. W. Gill, R. R. C., Superintendent, Nurses' Royal Infirmary, Edinburgh; Principal Matron, T. F. N. S.; President, Scottish Matrons' Association.

Miss Alicia Lloyd-Still, C. B. E., R. R. C., Head Matron. St. Thomas' Hospital; Superintendent, Florence Nightingale Nurses' Training School, London; Principal Matron. T. F. L. S., Fifth City of London General Hospital.

France

Countess De Roussy De Sales, Head Nurse of the Society « Secours aux Blessés Militaires », attached to the Field Service during the war.

Italy

Professor Lt. Col. Emilia Malatesta Anselmi, Volunteer Nurse "Grado Superiore" of Italian Red Cross; Appointed Inspector of Voluntary Nurses of Rome in 1911; General Assistant to H. R. H. the Duchess of Aosta, General Inspector of the Italian Red Cross nurses.

Countess Nerina Gigliucci, Volunteer Nurse "Grado Superiore" of Italian Red Cross; Chief of Nurses' Detachment to Ambulance 916, French Expeditionary Forces in Italy.

United States

Miss Carrie M. Hall, Superintendent of Nurses and Principal of School of Nurses of Peter Bent Brigham Hospital, Boston; Member of the National Committee, American Red Cross Nursing Service; Chief Nurse, American Red Cross in France.

Miss Julia Stimson, Chairman of Section on Nursing; Director, Army Nurse Corps, A. E. F., France.

Miss Lillian D. Wald, Founder and Head Resident Henry Street Settlement, New York; Representative of Federal Children's Bureau of Department of Labor, U.S.

Note

1 *Proceedings of the Medical Conference held at the Invitation of the Committee of Red Cross Societies, Cannes, France, April 1 to 11, 1919*, edited by the League of Red Cross Societies. (Geneva: League of Red Cross Societies, 1919), 5–11.

BIBLIOGRAPHY

Newspapers and Periodicals

British Medical Journal
International Journal of Public Health
International Review of the Red Cross
Journal de Genève
La Croix-Rouge Suisse. Revue mensuelle des Samaritains suisses, Soins des malades et hygiène populaire
Le Gaulois
Review and Information Bulletin
Science
The World's Health

References

Ador, Gustave. *Lettres à Germaine et à Frédéric Barbey, volume II: 1914–1928*, Françoise Dubosson et al. (ed.) Genève: Fondation Gustave Ador et Editions Slatkine, 2009.
Ambrosius, Lloyd E. *Wilsonianism: Woodrow Wilson and His Legacy in American Foreign Relations*. New York: Palgrave Macmillan, 2002.
Audoin-Rouzeau, Stéphane. *Combattre: une anthropologie historique de la guerre moderne, XIXe-XXIe siècle*. Paris: Seuil, 2008.
Bankers Trust Company. *Henry Pomeroy Davison: a Memorial*. New York: Bankers Trust Company, 1922.
Bankers Trust Company. *The Henry P. Davison Scholarships*. New York: Select Printing Company, 1927.
Barnett, Michael. *Empire of Humanity: A History of Humanitarianism*. Ithaca: Cornell University Press, 2011.
Bauer, Theodore J. 'Half a Century of International Control of the Venereal Diseases', *Public Health Reports (1896–1970)* 68, no. 8 (1953): 779–787.
Baughan, Emily. *Saving the Children. Humanitarianism, Internationalism, and Empire*. Berkeley: University of California Press, 2021.
Borowy, Iris. *Coming to Terms with World Health. The League of Nations Health Organisation 1921–1946*. Frankfurt am Main: Peter Lang, 2009.
Buckingham, Clyde E. *For Humanity's Sake: the Story of the Early Development of the League of Red Cross Societies*. Washington: Public Affairs Press, 1964.

Cabanes, Bruno. *The Great War and the Origins of Humanitarianism, 1914–1924*. Cambridge: Cambridge University Press, 2014.

Campbell, Kristine A. 'Knots in the Fabric: Richard Pearson Strong and the Bilibid Prison Vaccine Trials, 1905–1906', *Bulletin of the History of Medicine* 68, no. 4 (1994): 600–638.

Clarke, Walter. 'Venereal Diseases. A Challenge to the Red Cross', *Bulletin of the League of Red Cross Societies* 2, no. 4–5 (1921): 176–184.

Cotter, Cédric. *(S')Aider pour survivre. Action humanitaire et neutralité suisse pendant la Première Guerre mondiale*. Genève: Georg éditeur, 2017.

Cotter, Cédric. 'Red Cross'. In *1914–1918-online. International Encyclopedia of the First World War*, Ute Daniel, Peter Gatrell, Oliver Janz, Heather Jones, Jennifer Keene, Alan Kramer, and Bill Nasson (eds.). Berlin: Freie Universität Berlin, 2018.

Courmont, Juliette. *L'odeur de l'ennemi. L'imaginaire olfactif en 1914–1918*. Paris: Armand Colin, 2010.

Cueto, Marcos; Brown, Theodore M. and Fee, Elizabeth. *The World Health Organization: A History*. Cambridge: Cambridge University Press, 2019.

Dubin, Martin David. 'The League of Nations Health Organisation' in *International Health Organisations and Movements, 1918–1939*, Paul Weindling (ed.), 56–80. Cambridge: Cambridge University Press, 1995.

Dunant, Henry. *Un Souvenir de Solférino*. Genève: Imprimerie Jules-Guillaume Fick, 1862.

Durand, Roger. (ed.). *La Conférence Médicale de Cannes*. Genève: Société Henry Dunant, 1994.

Durand, Roger. (ed.). 'La Conférence médicale, ses participants et le Bulletin de la Ligue des Sociétés de la Croix-Rouge' in *La conférence médicale de Cannes*, 55–66. Geneva: Société Henry Dunant, 1994.

Ebeling, Richard M. 'William E. Rappard: An International Man in an Age of Nationalism', *The Freeman: Ideas on Liberty* 50, no. 1, online.

Evans, Jordan. 'New Blood: The role of the League of Red Cross Societies in the development of blood transfusion services from 1946–1979', PhD dissertation, Flinders University, 2024.

Farley, John. *To Cast Out Disease: A History of the International Health Division of the Rockefeller Foundation (1913–1951)*. New York: Oxford University Press, 2004.

Fathi, Romain and Oppenheimer, Melanie. 'The Shôken Fund and the evolution of the Red Cross movement', *European Review of History: Revue Européenne d'histoire* 30, no. 5 (2023): 812–831.

Fathi, Romain. 'Sovereignty, Democracy and Neutrality: French Foreign Policy and the National-Patriotic Humanitarianism of the French Red Cross, 1919–1928', *Contemporary European History* 32, no. 2 (2021): 305–323.

Fayet, Jean-François, Desgrandchamps, Marie-Luce, Cugnet, Marie, Hasler, et Donia (eds.). *La Croix face à l'Etoile Rouge: Humanitaire et Communisme au XXe siècle*. Geneva: Georg (forthcoming).

Fayet, Jean-François. 'D'une ambivalente hostilité à une distante adhésion: La Croix-Rouge soviétique et la Ligue des Sociétés de la Croix-Rouge durant l'entre-deux-guerre' in Jean-François Fayet, Marie-Luce Desgrandchamps, Marie Cugnet et Donia Hasler (eds.). *La Croix face à l'Etoile Rouge: Humanitaire et Communisme au XXe siècle*. Geneva: Georg (forthcoming).

Fayet, Jean-François. 'Humanitaire et Communisme: histoires parallèles et croisées' in Jean-François Fayet, Marie-Luce Desgrandchamps, Marie Cugnet et Donia Hasler, *La Croix face à l'Etoile Rouge: Humanitaire et Communisme au XXe siècle*. Geneva: Georg (forthcoming).

Forsythe, David P. 'The International Red Cross: Decentralization and its Effects', *Human Rights Quarterly* 40, no. 1 (2018): 61–90.
Guieu, Jean-Michel. *Le rameau et le glaive. Les militants français pour la Société des Nations*. Paris: Les Presses de Sciences Po, 2008.
Guillermand, Jean. 'La Croix-Rouge américaine et le corps médical français' in *La conférence médicale de Cannes*, Roger Durand (ed.). 99–118. Geneva: Société Henry Dunant, 1994.
Guthe, Thorstein. 'The International Union against the Venereal Diseases and the Treponematoses and the World Health Organisation', *The British Journal of Venereal Diseases* 36, no. 1 (1960): 4–6.
Hawgood, Barbara J. 'Doctor Albert Calmette 1863–1933: founder of antivenomous serotherapy and of antituberculous BCG vaccination', *Toxicon* 37, no. 9 (1999): 1241–1258.
Herrmann, Irène. 'Décrypter la concurrence humanitaire : le conflit entre Croix-Rouge(s) après 1918', *Relations internationales* 3, no. 151, (2012): 91–102.
Herrmann, Irène. 'Humanitaire et paix: une équation impossible?' in *Action humanitaire et quête de la Paix*, 29–45. Genève: Fondation Gustave Ador & Georg Editeur, 2018.
Herrmann, Irène. *L'humanitaire en questions: réflexions autour de l'histoire du Comité international de la Croix-Rouge*. Paris: Les Éditions du Cerf, 2018.
Hill, Claude H. 'The League of Red Cross Societies', *Bulletin of the Pan American Union* 57, no. 4 (1923): 323–326.
Howard-Jones, Norman. *International Public Health Between the Two World Wars. The Organisational Problems*. Geneva: World Health Organisation, 1978.
Howard-Jones, Norman. *Les bases scientifiques des Conférences sanitaires internationales 1851–1938*. Genève: Organisation Mondiale de la Santé, 1975.
Huber, Valeska. 'The Unification of the Globe by Disease? The International Sanitary Conferences on Cholera, 1851–1894', *The Historical Journal* 49, no. 2 (2006): 453–476.
Hutchinson, John F. *Champions of Charity: War and the Rise of the Red Cross*. Boulder: Westview Press, 1996.
Irwin, Julia 'The Disaster of War: American Understandings of Catastrophe, Conflict and Relief', *First World War Studies* 5, no. 1 (2014):17–28.
Irwin, Julia. *Making the World Safe. The American Red Cross and a Nation's Humanitarian Awakening*. Oxford: Oxford University Press, 2013.
Jones, Heather. 'International or transnational? Humanitarian action during the First World War', *European Review of History: Revue Européenne d'histoire* 16, no. 5 (2009): 697–713.
Lamont, Thomas W. *Henry P. Davison: the Record of a Useful Life*. New York: Harper, 1933.
League of Red Cross Societies (ed.). Proceedings of the Medical Conference held at the Invitation of the Committee of Red Cross Societies, Cannes, France, April 1 to 11, 1919. Geneva: League of Red Cross Societies, 1919.
Lowe, Kimberly A. 'The League of Red Cross Societies and International Committee of the Red Cross: a Re-Evaluation of American Influence in Interwar Internationalism', *Moving the Social* 57 (2017): 37–56.
Macleod, Roy. '*Scientists*' in *The Cambridge History of the First World War*, Jay Winter (ed.). 434–459. Cambridge: Cambridge University Press, 2014.
Macmillan, Margaret. *Paris 1919. Six Months the Changed the World*. London: John Murray, 2019.

Mahood, Linda. *Feminism and Voluntary Action: Eglantyne Jebb and Save the Children, 1876–1928*. Basingstoke: Palgrave Macmillan, 2009.

Manela, Erez. *The Wilsonian Moment. Self-Determination and the International Origins of Anticolonial Nationalism*. Oxford: Oxford University Press, 2007.

Mazower, Mark. *Governing the World. The History of an Idea, 1815 to the Present*. New York: Penguin Books, 2012.

McGuire, Michael E. 'At (Red) Cross Purposes: American Red Cross Humanitarian "Arrogance" and France's Great War Relief and Reconstruction, 1917–20', *European Review of History: Revue Européenne d'histoire* 30, no. 5 (2023): 705–726.

Menchik, Jeremy. 'Woodrow Wilson and the Spirit of Liberal Internationalism', *Politics, Religion & Ideology* 22, no. 2 (2021): 231–253.

Möller, Esther. 'Red Crescent (Hilal-i Ahmer)', in: *1914–1918-online. International Encyclopedia of the First World War*, Ute Daniel, Peter Gatrell, Oliver Janz, Heather Jones, Jennifer Keene, Alan Kramer, and Bill Nasson (eds.). Berlin: Freie Universität Berlin, 2019.

Moorehead, Caroline. *Dunant's Dream: War, Switzerland, and the History of the Red Cross*. New York: Carroll & Graf Publishers, 1999.

Naclerio, Richard A. *The Federal Reserve and Its Founders: Money, Politics and Power*. Newcastle upon Tyne: Agenda Publishing, 2018.

Oppenheimer, Melanie and Collins, Carolyn. *Henry Pomeroy Davison 1867–1922*. Geneva: Société Henry Dunant & International Federation of Red Cross and Red Crescent Societies, 2019.

Oppenheimer, Melanie. '"A golden moment?": The League of Red Cross Societies, the League of Nations and contested spaces of internationalism and humanitarianism, 1919–1922', in *League of Nations: Histories, legacies and impact*, Joy Damousi and Patricia O'Brien (eds.). 8–27. Melbourne: Melbourne University Press, 2018.

Oppenheimer, Melanie. 'Nurses of the League: the League of Red Cross Societies and the development of public health nursing post-WWI', *History Australia* 17, no. 4 (2020): 628–644.

Oppenheimer, Melanie; Schech, Susanne; Fathi, Romain; Wylie, Neville and Cresswell, Rosemary. 'Resilient Humanitarianism? Using Assemblage to re-evaluate the history of the League of Red Cross Societies', *The International History Review* 43, no. 3 (2021): 579–597.

Oppenheimer, Melanie; Wylie, Neville; Schech, Susanne Fathi, Romain and Evans, Jordan. *The League of Red Cross Societies and Twentieth-Century Humanitarianism*. Cambridge: Cambridge University Press, forthcoming.

Palmieri, Daniel. *Les Procès-Verbaux de l'Agence Internationale des Prisonniers de Guerre*, volume 2. *Genève: Comité International de la Croix-Rouge*, 2014.

Pedersen, Susan. 'Back to the League of Nations', *The American Historical Review* 112, no. 4 (2007): 1110–1112.

Piller, Elisabeth and Wylie, Neville. (eds.). *Humanitarianism and the Greater War 1914–24*. Manchester: Manchester University Press, 2023.

Reid, Daphne A. and Gilbo, Patrick F. *Beyond Conflict. The International Federation of the Red Cross and Red Crescent Societies, 1919–1994*. Geneva: IFRC, 1997.

Rodogno, Davide, Struck, Bernhard and Vogel, Jakob (eds.). *Shaping the Transnational Sphere: Experts, Networks, and Issues from the 1840s to the 1930s*. New York, Berghahn, 2015.

Rossini, Daniela. 'The Activity and Influence of the American Red Cross in Italy during and after World War One (1917–1919)', *European Review of History: Revue Européenne d'histoire* 30, no. 5, (2023): 685–704.

Silverman, Barry D. 'William Henry Welch (1850–1934): the road to Johns Hopkins', *Baylor University Medical Center Proceedings* 24, no. 3 (2011): 236–242.

Sluga, Glenda. *Internationalism in the Age of Nationalism*. Philadelphia, University of Pennsylvania Press, 2013.

Tapia, Claude and Taieb, Jacques. 'Conférences et Congrès Internationaux de 1815 à 1913', *Relations Internationales* 4, no. 5 (1976): 11–35.

Throntveit, Trygve. *Power without Victory. Woodrow Wilson and the American Internationalist Experiment*. Chicago: The University of Chicago Press, 2017.

Tooze, Adam. *The Deluge. The Great War and the Remaking of Global Order*. London: Allen Lane, 2014.

Towers, Bridget. 'Red Cross Organisational Politics, 1918–1922: Relations of Dominance and the Influence of the United States' in *International Health Organisations and Movements, 1918–1939*, Paul Weindling (ed.). 36–55. Cambridge: Cambridge University Press, 1995.

Weindling, Paul (ed.). *International Health Organisations and Movements, 1918–1939*. Cambridge: Cambridge University Press, 1995.

www.ingramcontent.com/pod-product-compliance
Lightning Source LLC
Chambersburg PA
CBHW030143170426
43199CB00008B/183